STUDY GUIDE/JOURNAL
—FOR USE WITH—
Why Shofars Wail
in Scripture and Today
The Exciting Stories—and Miracles!

Study Guide/Journal for use with Why Shofars Wail in Scripture and Today—
The Exciting Stories and Miracles!   By Mary A. Bruno, Ph.D.

i

Acknowledgments, permissions, and other credits:

Website design and maintenance by Michael and Michelle Lucas, Graphic Designers/Photographers; Web Options, LLC. www.weboptions.net.

Publication Date August 2016

Printed in the United States of America

Mary A. Bruno 2016

International Standard Book Number (ISBN): ISBN-13: 978-1535012584

International Standard Book Number (ISBN): ISBN-10: 1535012587

Create Space Independent Publishing Platform, North Charleston, SC.

International Standard Serial Number ISSN:

BISAC Category: REL006700 Religion/Biblical Studies/Bible Study Guides

Library of Congress Control Number: 2016910580

Dr. Mary A. Bruno, Vista, CA

Study Guide/Journal for use with Why Shofars Wail in Scripture and Today—
The Exciting Stories and Miracles!　　　　　By Mary A. Bruno, Ph.D.

ii

STUDY GUIDE/JOURNAL
—FOR USE WITH—
Why Shofars Wail
in Scripture and Today
The Exciting Stories—and Miracles!

By
Mary A. Bruno, Ph.D.
Vista, California

V89-100118-326P-111820

Study Guide/Journal for use with Why Shofars Wail in Scripture and Today—
The Exciting Stories and Miracles! By Mary A. Bruno, Ph.D.

iii

Study Guide/Journal for use with Why Shofars Wail in Scripture and Today—
The Exciting Stories and Miracles!   By Mary A. Bruno, Ph.D.

iv

About the Author

Mary A. Bruno, an ordained minister, serving with her husband, the Reverend Doctor Rocco Bruno, is Co-founder and Vice President of Interdenominational Ministries International, and Co-founder and Vice Chancellor of the IMI Bible College and Seminary in Vista, California, where she has taught for more than two decades. Her talks include humor, witty insights, and Scripture.

She has earned a Standard Ministerial Diploma from L.I.F.E. Bible College, a Doctor of Ministry Degree (D.Min.) from the School of Bible Theology; a Doctor of Theology Degree, Th.D.) from the IMI Bible College & Seminary; and a Doctor of Philosophy Degree in Pastoral Christian Counseling, (Ph.D.,P.C.C.) from the Evangelical Theological Seminary. The School of Bible Theology also awarded her an honorary Doctor of Divinity Degree, (D.D.).

Dr. Bruno has presented Spiritual Gift seminars, hosted retreats, and evangelized in the USA and abroad. Turnouts skyrocketed when she presided over the Vista Women's Aglow. Her "Words in Season" radio broadcast aired in the 1980's and 90's over KPRZ and KCEO in San Diego County.

For speaking engagements:
Email: imibcs@aol.com
Or write:

Dr. Mary A. Bruno
P.O. Box 2107
Vista, CA 92085–2107
United States of America

Study Guide/Journal for use with Why Shofars Wail in Scripture and Today—
The Exciting Stories and Miracles!   By Mary A. Bruno, Ph.D.

v

Study Guide/Journal for use with Why Shofars Wail in Scripture and Today—
The Exciting Stories and Miracles!   By Mary A. Bruno, Ph.D.

vi

To Father God and His dedicated kings and priests who faithfully study His Word, sound their shofars, and joyfully journal their spiritual insights and experiences.

Study Guide/Journal for use with Why Shofars Wail in Scripture and Today—
The Exciting Stories and Miracles!   By Mary A. Bruno, Ph.D.

How to Order *Why Shofars Wail in Scripture and Today—The Exciting Stories and Miracles!*

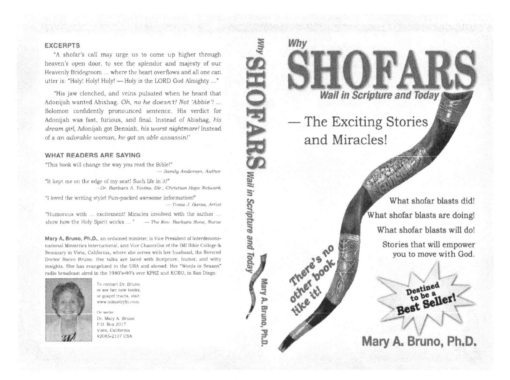

Why Shofars Wail in Scripture and Today—The Exciting Stories and Miracles!
Authored by Mary A. Bruno, Ph.D.

ISBN 9781533383020

To order this book, visit www.ministrylit.com. Dr. Bruno's books are also available at www.amazon.com

Also available in LARGE PRINT, and in Braille.
The Audio Version is coming soon.

Study Guide/Journal for use with Why Shofars Wail in Scripture and Today—
The Exciting Stories and Miracles!   By Mary A. Bruno, Ph.D.

How to Order This Book

To order this *STUDY GUIDE/JOURNAL*—FOR USE WITH—*Why Shofars Wail in Scripture and Today—The Exciting Stories and Miracles!* Authored by Mary A. Bruno, Ph.D., and to see her other publications, visit www.ministrylit.com. Dr. Bruno's books are also available at www.amazon.com

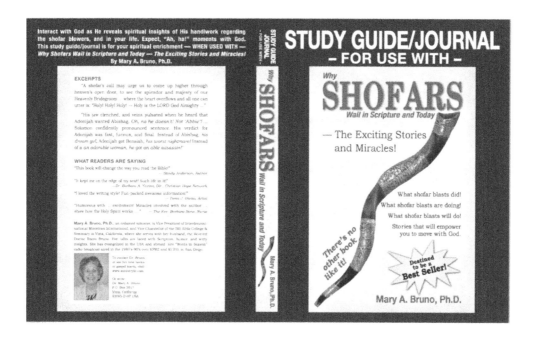

ISBN 9781535012584

See this book and Dr. Bruno's other writings, at www.ministrylit.com. Her books are also available at www.amazon.com.

Email: imibcs@aol.com

Write: **Dr. Mary A. Bruno**
            P.O. Box 2107
            Vista, California 92085-2107 United States of America

Study Guide/Journal for use with Why Shofars Wail in Scripture and Today—
The Exciting Stories and Miracles!   By Mary A. Bruno, Ph.D.

ix

Study Guide/Journal for use with Why Shofars Wail in Scripture and Today—
The Exciting Stories and Miracles!   By Mary A. Bruno, Ph.D.

x

Foreword

Israelites would soon hear the shofar again and would rejoice in its joyful sound. God was getting ready to unveil His generous new love token, *The Day of Jubilee!* On that great day, shofar blasts would ring throughout the land to announce release, restoration, and reconciliation with loved ones. God had already scheduled that exciting appointment on His calendar.[1]

As you read, *Why Shofars Wail in Scripture Today—The Exciting Stories and Miracles!,* you will continue to learn, to grow, and to experience the Wonders of our God. Your heart and soul will be touched in such a powerful way, that you will want to use this journal to study and secure the meanings, the lessons, and the very heart of God in His communication with mankind. This manual is perfect for private and corporate study. It can be used in small groups, churches, and in schools. God bless you as you deepen your faith to a new level in Him through the sound of the shofar as it reaches to heaven, and will someday be heard from heaven to earth.

Rev. Barbara A. Yovino, Ph.D.

Study Guide/Journal for use with Why Shofars Wail in Scripture and Today— The Exciting Stories and Miracles!   By Mary A. Bruno, Ph.D.

xi

Study Guide/Journal for use with Why Shofars Wail in Scripture and Today—
The Exciting Stories and Miracles!   By Mary A. Bruno, Ph.D.

xii

Acknowledgements

Many thanks to God's generous people who have helped to make this book a reality; especially <u>the Reverend Doctor Rocco Bruno</u>, my multi-talented, tri-lingual husband, a man of God, and missionary to Italy. His steady support is my treasure in his earthen vessel.

<u>The Reverend Shawn Brix,</u> of ReFrame Media, a division of Back to God Ministries International, Palos Heights, Illinois, has permitted the use of his article "The Final Sacrifice" that appeared in *Today* in March/April 2011, Vol. 62.[2] His aritcle was mentioned in chapter 28.

<u>Veronica Coenraad Jenks</u>, Director of KAIROS Resource Center at Eagles' Wings, taught me to blow a shofar. The first chapter tells how God used Veronica to affect my life.

<u>Lorri Jennex</u>, author, and business owner has shared writing tips, insights, and ongoing encouragement.[3]

<u>Kim Kinman,</u> Owner of KK Grafix, in Fallbrook, California, took my basic ideas and a shofar photo, and then applied her design skills and talents to transform them into the book cover.

<u>The Reverends Michael and Michelle Lucas</u>, of Web Options, LLC,[4] Oceanside, California, designed the website.[5]

<u>Bishop Robert Stearns</u>, Founder and Executive Director of Eagles' Wings, in Clarence, New York,[6] may not have known that his tremendously anointed ministry would stir my heart to move with God and a wailing shofar.

---

[2] http://today.reframemedia.com/archives/the-final-sacrifice-2011-04-22. See chapter 28 of this writing entitled, Shofar Blasts Predicted – Part 1

[3] lorri@lorrijennex.com
[4] www.weboptionsllc.com, mlucas@weboptions.net,   michellelucas@weboptions.net
[5] www.ministrylit.com

Study Guide/Journal for use with Why Shofars Wail in Scripture and Today—
The Exciting Stories and Miracles!   By Mary A. Bruno, Ph.D.

xiii

The Reverend Barbara Anne Yovino, Ph.D., has enriched this effort with her prayers and encouragement. She serves as Vice Pres. and Director of the Christian Hope Network, in Brooklyn, New York,[7] which has partnered with John Ramirez Ministries,[8] and Matt Sorger Ministries.[9] She is an Associate Pastor at Gateway City Church, in Brooklyn;[10] New York State Coordinator for the Day to Pray for the Peace of Jerusalem; New York Director of God.tv Prayer Line;[11] and Advisor for IMI Bible College & Seminary. She was right there in chapter one when this story began.

San Diego Christian Writers Guild (SDCWG). The San Marcos critique group is led by Barbara Waite, and includes Sandy Anderson, Jan Flickinger, and others, who have kindly shared valuable comments and suggestions.[12]

Others who have shared editorial comments and counsel: the Reverend Doctor Deone Gushwa; the Reverend Phadrae T. Halfacre; Pascal John Imperato, Author[13]; the Reverend Mary Anne Moyer.

Other Writers—Blessings to the many gifted writers whose books and websites (listed in the bibliography) have enhanced the research phase of this book. Any errors or omissions were purely unintentional. May God reward each person's labor for His glory.

Translations of the Holy Scriptures:

The *New King James Version* (NKJV) is the primary source of Scripture unless otherwise shown.

Scripture taken from the New King James Version. Copyright © 1982 by Thomas Nelson, Inc. Used by permission. All rights reserved.

Other translations that were cited when used:

---

[6] www.eagleswings.to
[7] www.chn.cc
[8] www.johnramirez.org
[9] www.mattsorger.com
[10] www.gatewaycitychurch.net
[11] www.god.tv
[12] http://sandiegocwg.com.
[13] JohnPascal.com

Study Guide/Journal for use with Why Shofars Wail in Scripture and Today—
The Exciting Stories and Miracles!   By Mary A. Bruno, Ph.D.

xiv

Mary A. Bruno, Ph.D.

Study Guide/Journal for use with Why Shofars Wail in Scripture and Today—The Exciting Stories and Miracles!   By Mary A. Bruno, Ph.D.

XV

Study Guide/Journal for use with Why Shofars Wail in Scripture and Today—
The Exciting Stories and Miracles!   By Mary A. Bruno, Ph.D.

xvi

Contents

*Study Guide/Journal for use with Why Shofars Wail in Scripture and Today—
The Exciting Stories and Miracles!*   By Mary A. Bruno, Ph.D.

Study Guide/Journal for use with Why Shofars Wail in Scripture and Today—
The Exciting Stories and Miracles!   By Mary A. Bruno, Ph.D.

xviii

Study Guide/Journal for use with Why Shofars Wail in Scripture and Today—
The Exciting Stories and Miracles!   By Mary A. Bruno, Ph.D.

xix

Study Guide/Journal for use with Why Shofars Wail in Scripture and Today—
The Exciting Stories and Miracles!   By Mary A. Bruno, Ph.D.

Preface

This study guide/journal, a companion to, *Why Shofars Wail in Scripture and Today—The Exciting Stories and Miracles!,* by Mary A. Bruno, Ph.D., was designed to help you recognize God's long-range plans and interaction with the shofar blowers in His Word, and in your life. Expect God to linger with you as He unfolds greater appreciation for how He grooms His servants for their callings, and then becomes their Secret Weapon in battle.

You will become familiar with every shofar blower and every shofar mention in Scripture, including a shofar-sound-alike voice, and what will happen when God's angels sound their shofars in the Book of Revelation.

Explore God's involvement in events that led to the shofar blasts, the miracles that followed, and what can happen for those who dare to blow a shofar today. You may even recognize some of God's plans and personal involvement that may have been overlooked your life.

"Ah, ha!" moments of will gladden your soul as God unveils His handiwork. Those sweet times may become your secret place of the Most High.

If not already in the habit of doing so, now would be a good time to start praying the following verse from God's Word—before attempting the chapter questions. Inviting God to join in your study may result in such joyous excitement that it might take a while to calm down after each discovery.

"Open my eyes, that I may see
Wondrous things from Your law."
(Psalm 119:18)

Mary A. Bruno, Ph.D.

Study Guide/Journal for use with Why Shofars Wail in Scripture and Today—
The Exciting Stories and Miracles!   By Mary A. Bruno, Ph.D.

1

Study Guide/Journal for use with Why Shofars Wail in Scripture and Today—
The Exciting Stories and Miracles!   By Mary A. Bruno, Ph.D.

Twenty–two Tips for Successful Bible Studies

1. **Pray privately**
   Ask God to help the leader (you?) to understand and teach what is on His heart for each class, to increase the spiritual growth of all who attend, and draw them closer to Him.

2. **Prepare a week or more before the first lesson**
   Read the entire textbook and answer the Study Guide/Journal questions for the first chapter.

3. **Meditate daily on the chapter's content**
   Ponder God's involvement with the people and events. Make notes about fresh insights.

4. **Review a day before the first class**
   Prayerfully review chapter one (or current chapter) from the textbook and your answers in this study guide/journal.

5. **Review an hour or more before the class**
   Prayerfully review the material and invite God's Presence direction before the first class starts.

6. **Prepare for the next lesson**
   The same day that a class is finished, is an ideal time to review the next chapter from the textbook and to write or consider the questions and answers for that chapter/class. This will provide time

Study Guide/Journal for use with Why Shofars Wail in Scripture and Today—
The Exciting Stories and Miracles! By Mary A. Bruno, Ph.D.

3

for God to expand the material and unfold spiritual applications that will help you to compare spiritual with spiritual and rightly apply His Word. Follow steps 1–5 for the next chapter(s).

7. **Before each session**

Ask God to help the leader (you?) to lead and guide the class according to His will, and for the participants to receive what they need to hear from the Lord.

8. **Welcome the participants with a smile and open each session with prayer:**

The following psalm shows how to approach the Lord in prayer. Notice His specific instructions, which show how to pray specific prayers.

> "Enter into His gates with thanksgiving,
> *And* into His courts with praise.
> Be thankful to Him, *and* bless His name.
> For the LORD *is* good;
> His mercy *is* everlasting,
> And His truth *endures* to all generations."
> (Psalm 100:–4–5)

a. **Thank God:**

While approaching the Lord, thank Him for Who He is and what He has done, including answered prayer.

b. **Praise God:**

Compliment God regarding who He is and what He has done. (Tell God what you like about Him.)

Study Guide/Journal for use with Why Shofars Wail in Scripture and Today—
The Exciting Stories and Miracles!   By Mary A. Bruno, Ph.D.

4

c. **Thank God again**

Acknowledge the Lord, and welcome His nearness.

d. **Bless God's name and acknowledge His greatness**

A list of 22 of God's names and definitions is provided to jog your memory regarding Who He is and what He does.

e. **Comment on God's goodness**

Ponder God's perfection and holiness, and mention specific areas of His goodness.

f. **Acknowledge God's mercy:**

Mention some of the times and ways that God has shown His kindness and tender compassion.

g. **Focus on God's truth**

Talk to God about His truth that is for all generations.

h. **Mention God's promises**

Remind God of His (specific) written promises that are still valid for all who believe. And then confidently apply them (claim them) when you pray.

9. **Present your requests**

After lingering with the Lord, pondering His greatness, and absorbing His loving kindness, would be a good time to ask Him to grant your requests.

10. **Start and finish on time**

Be punctual and stay on schedule, even if only one person is present. Waiting for the late comers encourages their tardiness

Study Guide/Journal for use with Why Shofars Wail in Scripture and Today—
The Exciting Stories and Miracles!   By Mary A. Bruno, Ph.D.

5

11. **Stay focused on the topic**

Avoid or redirect unrelated comments or trains of thought that can steer the lesson off course.

12. **The leader directs the class**

Do not permit members to usurp (take over) the leader's role. All must learn to follow before they can lead.

13. **Allow participants to share their comment(s)**

Never insist that anyone read or participate. Some may be illiterate shy, having a challenging day, etc.

14. **Affirm what others have said**

Be supportive and encouraging.

15. **Invite participants to speak up (briefly) as God leads**

Comments should emphasize or expand on a point(s) but not take over the class.

16. **Limit interruptions or distractions**

Courtesy calls for attention when someone speaks, reads, or prays. Discourage interruptions or engaging in other conversations while another is speaking or reading. Teach the class to harmonize softly as another prays, without drowning them out.

17. **Keep conversations positive and uplifting**

Redirect discussions that do not honor or glorify the Lord, to topics that edify.

Study Guide/Journal for use with Why Shofars Wail in Scripture and Today—
The Exciting Stories and Miracles!   By Mary A. Bruno, Ph.D.

6

18. Keep confidences private

Personal matters that have been shared within the group should not be discussed with others.

19. Avoid interrogations

Avoid questions that trigger painful memories and distance others. A parent, who has lost a child through death, legal ruling, etc., or a couple unable to conceive, may dread being asked their number of children. Other irritating questions include: "Did you find a job yet?" "Are you gaining weight?" "When are you getting married?" "Did you pass your test?" Others will tell you what they wish to share or discuss.

20. Ask,

"Do you wish to share anything with the group regarding what the Lord is doing in your life, or a prayer request?"

21. Avoid financial dealings

Financial transactions within the group can lead to disappointment, hurt feelings, broken fellowship, loss of friends, and affect one's relationship with God.

22. Conclude each session with a benediction (good word)

When one of God's servants leads a Bible-based class, he or she, may pronounce God's blessings upon His people. The following passage is a favorite among God's servants. [The actual benediction is in verses 24–26.]

"And the LORD spoke to Moses, saying:
"Speak to Aaron and his sons, saying,
'This is the way you shall bless the children of Israel. Say to them:

Study Guide/Journal for use with Why Shofars Wail in Scripture and Today—
The Exciting Stories and Miracles!   By Mary A. Bruno, Ph.D.

7

The LORD bless you and keep you;
The LORD make His face shine upon you,
And be gracious to you;
The LORD lift up His countenance upon you,
And give you peace.'"

"So they shall put My name on the children of Israel,
and I will bless them."

—Numbers 6:22–27, blank lines added

*Study Guide/Journal for use with Why Shofars Wail in Scripture and Today—
The Exciting Stories and Miracles!*   By Mary A. Bruno, Ph.D.

8

Twenty–two of God's Names and Definitions

1. *Elohim*—(plural), *Eloah* (singular) Strong and Mighty One (Gen. 1:1)

2. *El*— "God, god, mighty one, strength" (Deut. 32:4)

3. *El Elyon*—The Most High (Gen. 14:18–20)

4. *El Olam*—The Everlasting God (Gen. 21:33)

5. *El Shaddai*—The Almighty God (Gen 17:1)

6. *Adonai* (pl.)—Lord, lord, master, owner, ruler (Gen. 15:1, 2)

7. *Jehovah*—Personal NAME of God (Ex, 3:13–15)

8. *I AM*—The Eternally Existing One (John 8:58, 14:6, 8:12, 11:25

9. *Ha Tsur*—the Rock (Ex. 17:6; Deut. 32:4, 15, 18, 30, 31; Isa. 17:10; 26:10; 32:12; 51:1; Ps. 19:14; 1 Cor. 10:4.)

10. *Jehovah-Elohim*—The Triune God of Creation and Redeemer of His people (Gen. 2:4)

11. *Jehovah-Jireh*—The Lord Will Provide (Gen. 22:14, Rom. 8:32)

12. *Jehovah-Rapha*—I, the Lord, am your HEALER (Ex. 15:26, I Cor. 12:9.)

13. *Jehovah-Nissi*—The Lord is My Banner (Ex. 17:15, Ex. 17:8–15)

14. *Jehovah-Shalom*—The Lord is Peace (Judges 6:24, John 14:27, Eph. 2:15, 16)

15. *Jehovah-Raah*—The Lord is my Shepherd (Ps. 23:1, John 10:11, I Peter 5:4)

16. *Jehovah-Tsidkenu* The Lord Our Righteousness (Jer. 23:6, 1 Cor. 1:30)

Study Guide/Journal for use with Why Shofars Wail in Scripture and Today—
The Exciting Stories and Miracles!   By Mary A. Bruno, Ph.D.

9

17. *Jehovah-Sabaoth*—The Lord of Hosts, King of Glory (Psalm 24:10, 1 Sam. 1:3; 2 Kings 6:13–17)

18. *Jehovah-Shammah*—The Lord is There (Ez. 48:35, Heb. 13:5, 6)

19. *Theos*—The Word *[logos]* *(John 1:1)*. "The Greek word *theos,* like *elohim* can mean "God, or gods." It is the usual word for "God" in the New Testament."[14]

20. *Kurios*— Lord *[Kurios]* (Phil. 2:11). "And that every tongue should confess that Jesus Christ is Lord *[Kurios],* to the glory of God *[Theos]* the Father *[Pater]*" (Phil. 2:11). All three New Testament Divine names are used in the verse above. *Kurios* is like *Adonai* in the Old Testament."

21. *Pater*—Our Father *[Pater]* was used in the Lord's Prayer *(Matt. 6:9).*

22. *Abba*—(an Aramaic word)—Jesus used this word for "Father" when He prayed in the garden. It is also used regarding our adoption (placement as sons), which gives us the privilege of calling God "Father," *Abba (Father) (Rom. 8:15).*[15]

---

[14] *Foundations of Pentecostal Theology*, Guy P. Duffield/ N.M. Van Cleave, L.I.F.E. Bible College at Los Angeles, 1983, 1987, 2006, 2008.

[15] This list of God's names and their definitions was gleaned from: Chapter Two, The Doctrine of God, point IV., The Names of God, in the book entitled, *Foundations of Pentecostal Theology*, by Guy P. Duffield/N.M. Van Cleave, L.I.F.E. Bible College at Los Angeles, 1983, 1987, 2006, 2008, Foursquare Media, Los Angeles, CA.

Study Guide/Journal for use with Why Shofars Wail in Scripture and Today— The Exciting Stories and Miracles!   By Mary A. Bruno, Ph.D.

10

Chapter 1
The Call

Date: _____

The shofar was mentioned on textbook pages: 1, 2, 3, 4, 5, 6, 7, and 8.

Events or hurdles that you have faced while focusing on this chapter:

_____

_____

_____

_____

_____

_____

_____

_____

_____

___True: ___False:

Prior to attempting this chapter, I have asked God to give me new wisdom and understanding and to reveal all that I need to learn or change at this time.

Study Guide/Journal for use with Why Shofars Wail in Scripture and Today—
The Exciting Stories and Miracles!   By Mary A. Bruno, Ph.D.

POINTS TO PONDER: (Sharing your answers in class is always optional.)

1. Main characters: [Hint] Answers might include: God, Barbara, Mary, Rocco, Pastor Nasrallah, Eagles' Wings, Veronica Coenraad Jenks, shofar, etc.

_____

_____

_____

_____

2. Important or keywords: [One more hint to get started.] Answers might include: shofar, blasts, attraction, fear, risk, humiliation, wail, divine appointment, teach, research, blueletterbible.org, prophet, confirmed, blizzard, write, book, etc.

_____

_____

_____

_____

3. God had been working for at least eight years to help Mary attend the Eagles' Wings Conference where she heard wailing shofars. Please tell about when and how God may have worked in advance to position you for a _divine appointment._

_____

_____

_____

Study Guide/Journal for use with Why Shofars Wail in Scripture and Today—
The Exciting Stories and Miracles!   By Mary A. Bruno, Ph.D.

12

_____

_____

_____

_____

4. (Two–part Question) How did the shofar calls affect Mary when she was feeling spiritually weary? Explain if, how, and/or when a shofar's wail has affected you.

_____

_____

_____

_____

_____

_____

_____

5. (Two–part Question) Why did Mary hesitate to buy the shofar that kept tugging at her spirit? If that kind of reasoning has ever kept you from following through on what you believed to be God's leading, please explain.

_____

_____

_____

_____

_____

_____

Study Guide/Journal for use with Why Shofars Wail in Scripture and Today—
The Exciting Stories and Miracles! By Mary A. Bruno, Ph.D.

13

6. (Three-part Question) How might things have turned out if Veronica Coenraad Jenks had not shared instructions and information about the shofar? Do you think that she had any inkling of how God might use her casual conversation to affect Mary's life (and now, yours as well)? Discuss if or when you may have held back what you sensed God wanted you to say or do. (Sharing in class is optional.)

_____

_____

_____

_____

_____

_____

_____

_____

_____

7. (Two-part question). Discuss why the blizzard of the century that shut in everyone became a good or bad thing for Barbara and Mary. Tell about when God may have brought good from an unexpected change in your plans.

_____

_____

_____

_____

_____

_____

Study Guide/Journal for use with Why Shofars Wail in Scripture and Today—
The Exciting Stories and Miracles!   By Mary A. Bruno, Ph.D.

14

_____

_____

_____

_____

8. Discuss other biblical passages or memories that came to mind while studying this chapter, and what action(s) God may want you to take regarding them.

_____

_____

_____

_____

_____

_____

_____

_____

_____

_____

_____

9. Lessons learned, and insights or comments.

_____

_____

Study Guide/Journal for use with Why Shofars Wail in Scripture and Today—
The Exciting Stories and Miracles!　　　　　　By Mary A. Bruno, Ph.D.

15

_____

_____

_____

_____

_____

_____

_____

_____

_____

10. Improve your communication skills by summarizing this chapter in twenty–five meaningful words or less.

_____

_____

_____

_____

_____

_____

Dear God, I love and appreciate You because:

_____

_____

_____

_____

Study Guide/Journal for use with Why Shofars Wail in Scripture and Today—
The Exciting Stories and Miracles!   By Mary A. Bruno, Ph.D.

16

PRAYER REQUESTS/POTENTIAL MIRACLES:

Please review your prayer requests often and make marginal notes (with dates) of how and when God answered.

> "I will answer them before they even call to me.
> While they are still talking about their needs,
> I will go ahead and answer their prayers!"
> (Isaiah 65:24 New Living Translation (NLT))

_____

_____

_____

_____

_____

_____

_____

_____

_____

_____

_____

_____

_____

_____

_____

_____

_____

_____

_____

Study Guide/Journal for use with Why Shofars Wail in Scripture and Today—
The Exciting Stories and Miracles!   By Mary A. Bruno, Ph.D.

17

_____

_____

_____

_____

_____

_____

_____

_____

NOTES:

_____

_____

_____

_____

_____

Answers: Chapter 1

(The numbers in parentheses indicate where answers may be found in the textbook.

(pp. 1–3. (Opinion)

4. The shofar blasts were like floods of refreshing upon her spiritually dry ground.

(p. 2) (Opinion)

5. Mary struggled with the fear of failure. She knew people who had bought shofars, but could not blow them. (p. 4) (Opinion)

6. (Opinion) (pp. 3–5)

7. The delay positioned them to receive amazing prophetic words from God through Pastor Michael Nasrallah. (Opinion) (pp. 7–8)

8–10. (Opinion)

Study Guide/Journal for use with Why Shofars Wail in Scripture and Today—
The Exciting Stories and Miracles!   By Mary A. Bruno, Ph.D.

18

Chapter 2
Transformation

Date: _____

The shofar was mentioned on textbook pages: 9, 11, 12, and 14.

Events or hurdles that you have faced while focusing on this chapter:

_____

_____

_____

_____

_____

_____

_____

_____

___True: ___False:

Prior to attempting this chapter, I have asked God to give me new wisdom and understanding and to reveal all that I need to learn or change at this time.

Study Guide/Journal for use with Why Shofars Wail in Scripture and Today—
The Exciting Stories and Miracles!   By Mary A. Bruno, Ph.D.

19

POINTS TO PONDER: (Sharing your answers in class is always optional.)

1. Main characters:

_____

_____

_____

_____

2. Key words:

_____

_____

_____

_____

3. (Two-part question) Why might God permit someone to spend extended time in a difficult circumstance? Please write an example from the Scriptures or from your own experience, regarding going through spiritual "hot water."

_____

_____

_____

_____

_____

_____

_____

Study Guide/Journal for use with Why Shofars Wail in Scripture and Today—
The Exciting Stories and Miracles!   By Mary A. Bruno, Ph.D.

20

_____

_____

_____

4. (Two–part question) Explain why separation from the old head was necessary. Please write about if or when God has taken you through a separation process in order to break an attachment to someone or something, and what changed afterward.

_____

_____

_____

_____

_____

_____

_____

_____

_____

5. (Two–part question) What were the flesh probers after? Has God ever used one of His "flesh probers" to free you from something that needed to go? Please explain.

_____

_____

_____

_____

Study Guide/Journal for use with Why Shofars Wail in Scripture and Today—
The Exciting Stories and Miracles!   By Mary A. Bruno, Ph.D.

21

_____

_____

_____

_____

_____

_____

_____

6. (Three–part question) What was Shofie's most noticeable problem when she (the horn) was new? Discuss what helped. Explain how that kind of problem may apply to a believer's walk with God, and how He wants to help.

_____

_____

_____

_____

_____

_____

_____

_____

_____

_____

_____

_____

_____

Study Guide/Journal for use with Why Shofars Wail in Scripture and Today—
The Exciting Stories and Miracles!   By Mary A. Bruno, Ph.D.

22

7. (Two-part question) What may God want to accomplish when shakeups happen? Please write an example of when, how, and why God may have allowed a shakeup in your life, and what happened afterward.

_____

_____

_____

_____

_____

_____

_____

_____

_____

_____

_____

_____

_____

8. (Two-part question) Has God ever taken you through a spiritual buffing or polishing process? If so, please discuss what happened, how long it took, how you felt during the process, and what changed afterward.

_____

_____

_____

_____

Study Guide/Journal for use with Why Shofars Wail in Scripture and Today—
The Exciting Stories and Miracles!   By Mary A. Bruno, Ph.D.

23

_____

_____

_____

_____

_____

_____

9. Tell of other biblical passages or memories that God has brought to mind while reading this chapter, and how they relate to your life.

_____

_____

_____

_____

_____

_____

_____

10. Improve your communication skills by summarizing this chapter in twenty–five meaningful words or less.

_____

_____

_____

_____

_____

Study Guide/Journal for use with Why Shofars Wail in Scripture and Today—
The Exciting Stories and Miracles!   By Mary A. Bruno, Ph.D.

24

_____

_____

Dear God, I love and appreciate You because:

_____

_____

_____

PRAYER REQUESTS/POTENTIAL MIRACLES:

"I will answer them before they even call to me.
While they are still talking about their needs,
I will go ahead and answer their prayers!"
(Isaiah 65:24 NLT)

_____

_____

_____

_____

_____

_____

_____

_____

_____

_____

_____

_____

Study Guide/Journal for use with Why Shofars Wail in Scripture and Today—
The Exciting Stories and Miracles!   By Mary A. Bruno, Ph.D.

25

_____

_____

_____

_____

_____

_____

_____

_____

_____

_____

NOTES:

_____

_____

_____

Answers: Chapter 2

1–3. God may use difficult circumstances to help someone break free from an old attachment. (Opinion) (p. 9)

4. We, like the horn, must remove ourselves from the old head (power) in our life so that we can go forward with our new Master (God). (p. 11)

5. Flesh probers were after things from the past (flesh) that needed to go. (Opinion) (p. 10)

6. Shofie had a rotten stench from the residue of her past. A good cleansing helped. (p. 11)

7. God may use shakeups to reveal and release things that needed to be cleansed and removed (Opinion) (p.11)

8–10. (Opinion)

Study Guide/Journal for use with Why Shofars Wail in Scripture and Today—
The Exciting Stories and Miracles!   By Mary A. Bruno, Ph.D.

26

Chapter 3
The Message

Date: _____

The shofar was mentioned on textbook pages: 15, 16, 19, and 20.

Events or hurdles that you have faced while focusing on this chapter:

_____

_____

_____

_____

_____

_____

_____

_____

___True: ___False:

Prior to attempting this chapter, I have asked God to give me new wisdom and understanding and to reveal all that I need to learn or change at this time.

Study Guide/Journal for use with Why Shofars Wail in Scripture and Today—
The Exciting Stories and Miracles!   By Mary A. Bruno, Ph.D.

POINTS TO PONDER: (Sharing your answers in class is always optional.)

1. Main characters:

_____

_____

_____

_____

2. Key words:

_____

_____

_____

_____

3. A shofar's wail could issue a call to . . . . Explain why shofars sounded.

_____

_____

_____

_____

_____

_____

_____

_____

Study Guide/Journal for use with Why Shofars Wail in Scripture and Today—
The Exciting Stories and Miracles!   By Mary A. Bruno, Ph.D.

28

_____

_____

_____

_____

_____

4. (Two–part question) What circulated through the place where a horn (future shofar) attached to the old head? Explain how this kind of attachment was reminiscent of a believer's new attachment to Jesus Christ.

_____

_____

_____

_____

_____

_____

_____

_____

_____

_____

5. (Two–part question) Through whose seed did God say the Messiah would come? Explain how you think Eve felt about that, and why.

_____

_____

Study Guide/Journal for use with Why Shofars Wail in Scripture and Today—
The Exciting Stories and Miracles!   By Mary A. Bruno, Ph.D.

29

_____

_____

_____

_____

_____

_____

6. (Two–part question)

> "For **I *am* the** L<small>ORD</small>, **I** do **not change**;
> Therefore you are **not** consumed,
> O sons of Jacob" (Malachi 3:6).

What does God's plan (for the one by whom the Redeemer would come) reveal about His attitude toward those who have fallen into sin? What does the above passage tell us about the L<small>ORD</small>, who was merciful to Eve, and how He will deal with those from her bloodline who must live with the results of bad choices?

_____

_____

_____

_____

_____

_____

_____

_____

Study Guide/Journal for use with Why Shofars Wail in Scripture and Today—
The Exciting Stories and Miracles!   By Mary A. Bruno, Ph.D.

30

7. (Two-part question) What are the sounds and messages of the following shofar blasts?

Tekiah:

_____

_____

_____

_____

_____

_____

_____

Shevarim:

_____

_____

_____

_____

_____

_____

_____

Study Guide/Journal for use with Why Shofars Wail in Scripture and Today—
The Exciting Stories and Miracles!   By Mary A. Bruno, Ph.D.

31

8. (Three–part question) Discuss the sounds and messages of the following blasts:

Teruah :

_____

_____

_____

_____

_____

_____

_____

_____

Shevarim Teruah:

_____

_____

_____

_____

_____

_____

_____

_____

Study Guide/Journal for use with Why Shofars Wail in Scripture and Today—
The Exciting Stories and Miracles!   By Mary A. Bruno, Ph.D.

32

Tekiah Gedolah:

_____

_____

_____

_____

_____

_____

_____

9. Lessons learned from this chapter or a special insight(s) into God's loving and forgiving involvement with His people.

_____

_____

_____

_____

_____

_____

_____

_____

_____

_____

_____

_____

_____

Study Guide/Journal for use with Why Shofars Wail in Scripture and Today—
The Exciting Stories and Miracles!   By Mary A. Bruno, Ph.D.

33

10. Improve your communication skills by summarizing this chapter in twenty–five meaningful words or less.

_____

_____

_____

_____

_____

Dear God, I love and appreciate You because:

_____

_____

_____

_____

PRAYER REQUESTS/POTENTIAL MIRACLES:

"I will answer them before they even call to me.
While they are still talking about their needs,
I will go ahead and answer their prayers!"
(Isaiah 65:24 NLT)

_____

_____

_____

Study Guide/Journal for use with Why Shofars Wail in Scripture and Today—
The Exciting Stories and Miracles!   By Mary A. Bruno, Ph.D.

34

_____

_____

_____

_____

_____

_____

_____

_____

_____

_____

_____

_____

_____

_____

_____

_____

_____

_____

_____

_____

_____

_____

_____

_____

_____

Study Guide/Journal for use with Why Shofars Wail in Scripture and Today—
The Exciting Stories and Miracles! By Mary A. Bruno, Ph.D.

35

NOTES:

_____

_____

_____

_____

_____

Answers: Chapter 3

1–2. (Opinion)

3. A shofar could issue a call to worship, announce God's Presence, summon to battle, sound an alarm, declare a new king, and proclaim a fast, a feast, or freedom. (Opinion) (p. 15.)

4. The horn's attachment and our salvation (attachment to our new Head) both involved blood. (Opinion) (pp. 16–17)

5. The Redeemer—Messiah—would come through Eve's seed. She must have been very relieved. (p. 16)

6. God is unchanging and merciful. (Opinion) Malachi 3:6. Jesus the Messiah is able to rescue us from our sins, failures, and bad choices. (pp. 18–19)

7. The Tekiah: is one long blast that reminds hearers that the LORD God is one God.

   The Shevarim is a wailing blast, repeated three times; and is likened to a sad heart that longs to return to God. (p. 19).

8. The Teruah has nine rapid short blasts in groups of three that sounds an alarm, wake up call, jubilee blessings, and joy. (p. 19)

   The Shevarim Teruah has three wailing blasts followed by nine staccato blasts and is said to open the heavens. (p. 19)

   The Tekiah Gedolah, the Great Blast or Great Tekiah, has one very long unbroken blast that urges to praise the Creator. It also, announces His presence or His coming. (p. 20)

9. (Opinion)

10. Summary

Study Guide/Journal for use with Why Shofars Wail in Scripture and Today—
The Exciting Stories and Miracles!   By Mary A. Bruno, Ph.D.

36

Chapter 4

Religious Error

Date: _____

The shofar was mentioned on textbook pages: 21 and 27.

Events or hurdles that you have faced while focusing on this chapter:

_____

_____

_____

_____

_____

_____

_____

_____

_____

___True: ___False:

Prior to attempting this chapter, I have asked God to give me new wisdom and understanding and to reveal all that I need to learn or change at this time.

Study Guide/Journal for use with Why Shofars Wail in Scripture and Today—
The Exciting Stories and Miracles!   By Mary A. Bruno, Ph.D.

37

POINTS TO PONDER: (Sharing your answers in class is always optional.)

1. Main characters:

_____

_____

_____

_____

2. Key words:

_____

_____

_____

_____

3. In this chapter the shofar wails were God's love calls for His people to hear and obey His message, and to recognize His anointed leader. They called to give up idolatry, make God King, and enjoy His protection and provision.

(Three–part question) Why may God have used so many plagues and miracles that were linked to Egypt's objects of worship? Has God ever allowed someone or something that you adored, to fall? If so, how did that affect your relationship with God and him/her/it/or them?

_____

_____

_____

_____

Study Guide/Journal for use with Why Shofars Wail in Scripture and Today—
The Exciting Stories and Miracles! By Mary A. Bruno, Ph.D.

38

_____

_____

_____

_____

_____

_____

4. (Two–part question) How do you think God feels about people who are involved in religions that worship idols? Please comment on John 3:16–17 and Romans 10:9–12.

_____

_____

_____

_____

_____

_____

_____

5. (Four–part question) Are you relying more on people or things to meet your needs, instead of trusting in God? If so, how do you think the Lord feels about that? Do you need to change anything? Why?

_____

_____

_____

Study Guide/Journal for use with Why Shofars Wail in Scripture and Today—
The Exciting Stories and Miracles!   By Mary A. Bruno, Ph.D.

39

_____

_____

_____

_____

_____

_____

_____

"I will dwell in them
And walk among them.
I will be their God,
And they shall be My people."
Therefore
"Come out from among them
And be separate, says the Lord.
Do not touch what is unclean,
And I will receive you."
"I will be a Father to you,
And you shall be My sons and daughters,
Says the LORD Almighty."

—2 Corinthians 6:14b–18

According to God's Word, I will trust Him to help me to . . .

_____

_____

_____

_____

_____

Study Guide/Journal for use with Why Shofars Wail in Scripture and Today—
The Exciting Stories and Miracles!   By Mary A. Bruno, Ph.D.

40

6. How has the information from this chapter affected the way that you view the spiritual needs of people in other religions? Please explain

_____

_____

_____

_____

_____

7. Lessons learned about God's loving involvement with His people.

_____

_____

_____

_____

_____

_____

8. Are you ready to commit (by God's grace) to address, change, or make more room for more of His loving presence and good plans for your life? Please explain:

_____

_____

_____

_____

_____

Study Guide/Journal for use with Why Shofars Wail in Scripture and Today— The Exciting Stories and Miracles!   By Mary A. Bruno, Ph.D.

41

_____

_____

_____

9. Is there anything else that you need to discuss with God? Please Explain:

_____

_____

_____

_____

_____

_____

_____

_____

_____

10. Improve your communication skills by summarizing this chapter in twenty–five meaningful words or less.

_____

_____

_____

_____

_____

_____

_____

Study Guide/Journal for use with Why Shofars Wail in Scripture and Today—
The Exciting Stories and Miracles!   By Mary A. Bruno, Ph.D.

42

Dear God, I love and appreciate You because:

_____

_____

_____

PRAYER REQUESTS/POTENTIAL MIRACLES:

"I will answer them before they even call to me.
While they are still talking about their needs,
I will go ahead and answer their prayers!"
(Isaiah 65:24 NLT)

_____

_____

_____

_____

_____

_____

_____

_____

_____

_____

_____

_____

_____

*Study Guide/Journal for use with Why Shofars Wail in Scripture and Today—
The Exciting Stories and Miracles!*   By Mary A. Bruno, Ph.D.

43

_____

_____

_____

_____

_____

NOTES:

_____

_____

_____

_____

Answers: Chapter 4

1–2. (Opinion)

3. God probably used plagues to expose Egypt's mistaken trust in false gods. (p. 21)

Hapil could not give clean water. Jesus is the Living Water. (p. 22)

Hecket was supposed to be a part frog and part woman, but she could not help expectant mothers to bring forth a new life. The Lord made all of the creation, creatures, and all life. He could have helped. (p. 22)

Their "Super Fly" could not help. God is a sun and shield, and will give grace and glory, and withhold no good thing from them who walk uprightly. (p. 23)

Nevis could not help their cattle, but God could prosper in all that they did. (pp. 23–24)

God (Who never changes) forgives all of our sins and heals all of our diseases. (p. 25)

God may have sent the plagues to show the Egyptians they had believed lies, to expose them to the truth of Who He is, and to show how He could help them. (pp. 26–27).

4–10. (Opinion)

Study Guide/Journal for use with Why Shofars Wail in Scripture and Today—
The Exciting Stories and Miracles!   By Mary A. Bruno, Ph.D.

44

Chapter 5
Impossibilities

Date: _____

The shofar was mentioned on textbook page: 34.

Events or hurdles that you have faced while focusing on this chapter:

_____

_____

_____

_____

_____

_____

_____

_____

_____

___True: ___False:

Prior to attempting this chapter, I have asked God to give me new wisdom and understanding and to reveal all that I need to learn or change at this time.

Study Guide/Journal for use with Why Shofars Wail in Scripture and Today—
The Exciting Stories and Miracles!   By Mary A. Bruno, Ph.D.

45

POINTS TO PONDER: (Sharing your answers in class is always optional.)

1. Main characters:

_____

_____

_____

_____

2. Key words:

_____

_____

_____

_____

3. (Two-part question) What made the Red Sea's waters stand upright in a heap? Can you tell of a time when you saw or experienced a miracle of God?

_____

_____

_____

_____

_____

_____

_____

Study Guide/Journal for use with Why Shofars Wail in Scripture and Today—
The Exciting Stories and Miracles!   By Mary A. Bruno, Ph.D.

46

4. How many women do you suppose were included in "all the women" who joined Miriam with timbrels (tambourines) and danced in her victory celebration?

_____

_____

_____

_____

5. What are God's "If" conditions and promises in Exodus 19:4–6?

_____

_____

_____

_____

_____

_____

_____

_____

_____

_____

_____

Study Guide/Journal for use with Why Shofars Wail in Scripture and Today—
The Exciting Stories and Miracles!   By Mary A. Bruno, Ph.D.

47

_____

_____

6. (Three–part question) Explain why God disclosed His assets and pledged His love to His people. Do you think He was bragging when He went public regarding His possessions (net worth)? How did God's motivations for doing so, and the results differ from those of Hezekiah in 2 Kings 20:12–19?

_____

_____

_____

_____

_____

_____

_____

_____

_____

7. Please give a few reasons for why God came to the people in a cloud in Exodus 19:9. Can you mention any other times that God appeared in a cloud?

_____

_____

_____

_____

_____

_____

Study Guide/Journal for use with Why Shofars Wail in Scripture and Today—
The Exciting Stories and Miracles!   By Mary A. Bruno, Ph.D.

48

_____

_____

_____

_____

8. What kind of "horn" was the trumpet that sounded long in Exodus 19:13, and what was its message?

_____

_____

_____

_____

_____

_____

_____

_____

9. Lessons learned, and insights or comments regarding this chapter.

_____

_____

_____

_____

_____

_____

_____

_____

Study Guide/Journal for use with Why Shofars Wail in Scripture and Today—
The Exciting Stories and Miracles!   By Mary A. Bruno, Ph.D.

49

_____

_____

_____

_____

_____

_____

_____

10. Improve your communication skills by summarizing this chapter in twenty–five meaningful words or less.

_____

_____

_____

_____

_____

_____

Dear God, I love and appreciate You because:

_____

_____

_____

_____

_____

Study Guide/Journal for use with Why Shofars Wail in Scripture and Today—
The Exciting Stories and Miracles!   By Mary A. Bruno, Ph.D.

50

PRAYER REQUESTS/POTENTIAL MIRACLES:

"I will answer them before they even call to me.
While they are still talking about their needs,
I will go ahead and answer their prayers!"
(Isaiah 65:24 NLT)

_____

_____

_____

_____

_____

_____

_____

_____

_____

_____

_____

_____

_____

_____

_____

_____

_____

_____

Study Guide/Journal for use with Why Shofars Wail in Scripture and Today—
The Exciting Stories and Miracles!   By Mary A. Bruno, Ph.D.

_____

_____

_____

_____

_____

NOTES:

_____

_____

_____

_____

Answers: Chapter 5

3. (Opinion) God congealed them. (Opinion) (p. 29)

4. (Opinion) There must have been thousands of rejoicing women. (p. 30)

5. If: you obey My voice, and keep My covenant, then you shall be a special treasure to Me above all people... And you shall be to Me a kingdom of priests and a holy nation (Ex. 19:4–6). (p. 32)

6. God disclosed His assets to prove that He could take care of His people). (Opinion) (p. 33) Hezekiah may have been trying to impress his guests.

7. (Opinion) God came in a visible cloud so the people would know that He was with Moses, that He had appointed Moses to lead them; and so they would believe Moses forever (p. 33). (Opinion) God also manifested His Presence by the cloud that was over the tabernacle; and when He led by a cloud by day, and by the appearance of fire by night. In Acts 1:9, a cloud received Jesus—Yeshua, the Messiah—40 days after he had risen from the dead.

8. The horn was a _yowbel,_ a ram's horn shofar. (p. 34) The shofar called to come to the mountain where God was. It called to come closer to God.

9–10. (Opinion)

Study Guide/Journal for use with Why Shofars Wail in Scripture and Today—
The Exciting Stories and Miracles!   By Mary A. Bruno, Ph.D.

52

Chapter 6

What a Blast!

Date_____

The shofar was mentioned on textbook pages: 35, 36, and 37.

Events or hurdles that you have faced while focusing on this chapter:

_____

_____

_____

_____

_____

_____

_____

_____

___True: ___False:

Prior to attempting this chapter, I have asked God to give me new wisdom and understanding and to reveal all that I need to learn or change at this time.

Study Guide/Journal for use with Why Shofars Wail in Scripture and Today—
The Exciting Stories and Miracles!   By Mary A. Bruno, Ph.D.

POINTS TO PONDER: (Sharing your answers in class is always optional.)

1. Main characters:

_____

_____

_____

_____

2. Key words:

_____

_____

_____

_____

3. What are your thoughts regarding the origin of the first shofar?

_____

_____

_____

_____

_____

_____

_____

_____

Study Guide/Journal for use with Why Shofars Wail in Scripture and Today—
The Exciting Stories and Miracles! By Mary A. Bruno, Ph.D.

54

4. Explain why the evil one may tremble when he hears a shofar's wail.

_____

_____

_____

_____

_____

_____

5. Who do you think blew that first shofar in Scripture? Why?

_____

_____

_____

_____

_____

_____

_____

6. What happened when the first recorded shofar's sound waves in Scripture rippled through the Israelites' camp on their third day at the base of Mount Sinai? Please explain if you have ever had a startling, noisy, or earthshaking wake up call.

_____

_____

Study Guide/Journal for use with Why Shofars Wail in Scripture and Today—
The Exciting Stories and Miracles!   By Mary A. Bruno, Ph.D.

55

_____

_____

_____

_____

_____

_____

_____

_____

_____

7. Why do you think God found it necessary to include, "You shall not make *anything to be* with Me—gods of silver or gods of gold you shall not make for yourselves" (Ex. 20:23)? Explain how God must feel when His people honor or rely on dead people, statues, religious images, medals, people, etc., for comfort or help, instead of going directly to Him.

_____

_____

_____

_____

_____

_____

_____

_____

_____

Study Guide/Journal for use with Why Shofars Wail in Scripture and Today—
The Exciting Stories and Miracles!　　　　　By Mary A. Bruno, Ph.D.

56

8. (Four–part question)

"In every place where I record My name I will come to you, and I will bless you" (2 Kings 20:24b).

What does God promise to do for His people wherever His name is recorded and remembered? Does that promise apply to believers today? Is God's name honored or recorded in your home? If it is, explain in what way(s) and what this means for you and your family.

_____

_____

_____

_____

_____

_____

_____

_____

_____

_____

_____

_____

_____

_____

Study Guide/Journal for use with Why Shofars Wail in Scripture and Today—
The Exciting Stories and Miracles!   By Mary A. Bruno, Ph.D.

57

_____

_____

_____

_____

9. ____True, ____False:

God is pleased with the things that are said, done, or displayed in my home (including my vehicle), and with what comes in by way of the radio, Internet, television, visitors, and what is shared on the telephone, computer, electronic device, etcetera.

10. Improve your communication skills by summarizing this chapter in twenty–five meaningful words or less.

_____

_____

_____

_____

_____

_____

Dear God, I love and appreciate You because:

_____

_____

_____

_____

Study Guide/Journal for use with Why Shofars Wail in Scripture and Today—
The Exciting Stories and Miracles!   By Mary A. Bruno, Ph.D.

58

PRAYER REQUESTS/POTENTIAL MIRACLES:

"I will answer them before they even call to me.
While they are still talking about their needs,
I will go ahead and answer their prayers!"
(Isaiah 65:24 NLT)

_____

_____

_____

_____

_____

_____

_____

_____

_____

_____

_____

_____

_____

_____

_____

_____

_____

_____

_____

Study Guide/Journal for use with Why Shofars Wail in Scripture and Today—
The Exciting Stories and Miracles! By Mary A. Bruno, Ph.D.

59

_____

_____

_____

_____

_____

_____

_____

NOTES:

_____

_____

_____

_____

Answers: Chapter 6

1–3. (Opinion) (pp. 35-36)

4. The evil one may think the Lord has returned and that his (Satan's) time on earth is over and it is time for him to face his doom and serve his sentence. (p. 36)

5. (Opinion) God probably blew that shofar, because He is the only one mentioned as being on that mountain when the shofar wailed. (p. 37)

6. The people shook with holy terror. (p. 37)

7. Before they left Egypt, the Israelites had seen their captors worship idols (From the previous chapter) (p. 33,). God does not like it, and will know that He is not a person's first choice for assistance when someone prays to something, or to someone other than Himself. (Opinion) (p.39)

8. God blesses all who are where His name is recorded and remembered, which includes us. See Ex. 20:25b. (Opinion) (p. 39)

9–10. (Opinion)

Study Guide/Journal for use with Why Shofars Wail in Scripture and Today—
The Exciting Stories and Miracles!   By Mary A. Bruno, Ph.D.

60

Chapter 7
The Ark of God's Covenant

Date: _____

The shofar was mentioned on textbook pages: 41, 42, 43, 44, and 46.

Events or hurdles that you have faced while focusing on this chapter:

_____
_____
_____
_____
_____
_____
_____
_____
_____

___True: ___False:

Prior to attempting this chapter, I have asked God to give me new wisdom and understanding and to reveal all that I need to learn or change at this time.

Study Guide/Journal for use with Why Shofars Wail in Scripture and Today—
The Exciting Stories and Miracles!   By Mary A. Bruno, Ph.D.

61

POINTS TO PONDER: (Sharing your answers in class is always optional.)

1. Main characters:

_____

_____

_____

_____

2. Key words:

_____

_____

_____

_____

3. What do you think Moses' tiny ark, the Ark of the Covenant, the reeds in the water, Moses' rod of leadership, and the Red Sea, pictured regarding God's long-term plans, protection, and provision?

_____

_____

_____

_____

_____

_____

_____

Study Guide/Journal for use with Why Shofars Wail in Scripture and Today—
The Exciting Stories and Miracles!   By Mary A. Bruno, Ph.D.

62

_____

_____

_____

4. Can you share an example of how the following Scripture has proven true in your life, or for someone in the Bible?

"And we know that all things work together for good to those who love God, to those who are the called according to *His* purpose" (Romans 8:28).

_____

_____

_____

_____

_____

_____

_____

_____

_____

5. (Two–part question) What did God engrave while on the mountain, and how did the results affect His people? What did Aaron (the priest) engrave while in the valley, and how did his results affect the people's relationship with God?

_____

_____

Study Guide/Journal for use with Why Shofars Wail in Scripture and Today—
The Exciting Stories and Miracles!   By Mary A. Bruno, Ph.D.

63

_____

_____

_____

_____

_____

_____

_____

6. (Two-part question) What kinds of sounds rang out when it was time for the Ark of the Covenant (symbol of God's Presence) to move? Do you think those sounds could still alert God's people that He is moving among us?

_____

_____

_____

_____

_____

7. (Three-part question) From what place did God speak intimately? Explain how that place of communication compares with the believer's place of meeting with God. What kind of welcome can we expect when we enter into our secret place (spiritual place) with the Lord?

_____

_____

_____

_____

Study Guide/Journal for use with Why Shofars Wail in Scripture and Today—
The Exciting Stories and Miracles!   By Mary A. Bruno, Ph.D.

64

_____

_____

_____

_____

_____

_____

_____

8. Would you like to play with any of God's cherubim or bounce them on your knees? Why?

_____

_____

_____

_____

_____

9. Explain the veil of the temple's symbolism.

_____

_____

_____

_____

_____

_____

Study Guide/Journal for use with Why Shofars Wail in Scripture and Today—
The Exciting Stories and Miracles!   By Mary A. Bruno, Ph.D.

65

_____

_____

_____

_____

_____

_____

_____

_____

_____

10. Improve your communication skills by summarizing this chapter in twenty–five meaningful words or less.

_____

_____

_____

_____

_____

_____

Dear God, I love and appreciate You because:

_____

_____

_____

Study Guide/Journal for use with Why Shofars Wail in Scripture and Today—
The Exciting Stories and Miracles! By Mary A. Bruno, Ph.D.

66

PRAYER REQUESTS/POTENTIAL MIRACLES:

"I will answer them before they even call to me.
While they are still talking about their needs,
I will go ahead and answer their prayers!"
(Isaiah 65:24 NLT)

_____

_____

_____

_____

_____

_____

_____

_____

_____

_____

_____

_____

_____

_____

_____

_____

_____

_____

_____

Study Guide/Journal for use with Why Shofars Wail in Scripture and Today—
The Exciting Stories and Miracles!   By Mary A. Bruno, Ph.D.

67

_____

_____

_____

NOTES:

_____

_____

_____

_____

Answers: Chapter 7

1–2. (Opinion)

3. Moses' ark, etc., hinted of God's rescue plan for Moses to lead the Israelites through a larger body of water. (p. 41)

4. (Opinion).

5. Our loving God engraved what the people _needed_—His Word—The Ten Commandments—which gave the people direction and helped them to walk closely with Him. Aaron engraved what the people _wanted_ (a handsome idol) that redirected their hearts and affection away from God. (p. 42)

6. Shofars sounded on the Ark of the Covenant's moving day. (p. 42) (Opinion)

7. God spoke from above the mercy seat between the cherubim's wings. We can expect mercy when we enter into God's Presence. (p. 42). (Opinion)

8. Cherubim are God's armed guards. (pp. 42–43)

9. The thick veil of the temple hung from metal clasps, affixed to acacia wood. It was a type of Christ's body that was fastened with metal spikes to the cross. While Jesus—The Messiah—hung suspended between heaven and earth, He bore our sins and became the Way for us to be reunited with God. The veil was the way into the Holy of Holies and communion with God. Believers enter in now through faith in Jesus (Yeshua). He is the only Way that we may enter into God's presence. (p. 46)

10. (Opinion)

Study Guide/Journal for use with Why Shofars Wail in Scripture and Today—
The Exciting Stories and Miracles!   By Mary A. Bruno, Ph.D.

68

Chapter 8
Moving With God—Part 1

Date_____

The shofar was mentioned on textbook page: 50, 51, and 52.

Events or hurdles that you have faced while focusing on this chapter:

_____

_____

_____

_____

_____

_____

_____

_____

_____

___True: ___False:

Prior to attempting this chapter, I have asked God to give me new wisdom and understanding and to reveal all that I need to learn or change at this time.

Study Guide/Journal for use with Why Shofars Wail in Scripture and Today—
The Exciting Stories and Miracles!   By Mary A. Bruno, Ph.D.

69

POINTS TO PONDER: (Sharing your answers in class is always optional.)

1. Main characters:

_____

_____

_____

_____

2. Key words:

_____

_____

_____

_____

3. (Four–part question) What happened when Aaron's sons, Nadab and Abihu, offered unholy fire on God's Holy Altar? Do you think they knew better than to do what they did? Explain why. Write Proverbs 29:1

_____

_____

_____

_____

_____

_____

_____

Study Guide/Journal for use with Why Shofars Wail in Scripture and Today—
The Exciting Stories and Miracles!   By Mary A. Bruno, Ph.D.

70

_____

_____

_____

_____

_____

4. Who or what did God's fire burn in Numbers chapter 11?

_____

_____

_____

_____

_____

5. Explain what the two silver trumpet blasts signaled.

_____

_____

_____

_____

_____

_____

_____

Study Guide/Journal for use with Why Shofars Wail in Scripture and Today—
The Exciting Stories and Miracles!   By Mary A. Bruno, Ph.D.

71

_____

_____

_____

6. Why does Numbers 10:9 say to sound the alarm with trumpets (clap, sing, and shout praises to God) *before* facing an enemy?

_____

_____

_____

_____

_____

7. How do you think the enemy feels when he hears God's people blowing silver trumpets or clapping, singing, and shouting praises to God?

_____

_____

_____

_____

_____

8. Comment on some of your experiences that involved moving with God.

_____

_____

Study Guide/Journal for use with Why Shofars Wail in Scripture and Today—
The Exciting Stories and Miracles!   By Mary A. Bruno, Ph.D.

72

_____

_____

_____

_____

_____

_____

_____

_____

9. Write Isaiah 59:19. When under spiritual attack, and/or when praying for others, I will . . . , and will also trust God to . . . .

_____

_____

_____

_____

_____

_____

_____

_____

_____

_____

_____

Study Guide/Journal for use with Why Shofars Wail in Scripture and Today—
The Exciting Stories and Miracles!   By Mary A. Bruno, Ph.D.

73

_____

_____

_____

_____

_____

10. Improve your communication skills by summarizing this chapter in twenty–five meaningful words or less.

_____

_____

_____

_____

_____

_____

_____

Dear God, I love and appreciate You because:

_____

_____

_____

_____

_____

_____

Study Guide/Journal for use with Why Shofars Wail in Scripture and Today—
The Exciting Stories and Miracles!   By Mary A. Bruno, Ph.D.

74

PRAYER REQUESTS/POTENTIAL MIRACLES:

"I will answer them before they even call to me.
While they are still talking about their needs,
I will go ahead and answer their prayers!"
(Isaiah 65:24 NLT)

_____

_____

_____

_____

_____

_____

_____

_____

_____

_____

_____

_____

_____

_____

_____

_____

_____

Study Guide/Journal for use with Why Shofars Wail in Scripture and Today—
The Exciting Stories and Miracles!   By Mary A. Bruno, Ph.D.

75

_____

_____

_____

_____

NOTES:

_____

_____

_____

_____

Answers: Chapter 8

1–2. (Opinion)

3. Fire came out from before the Lord and snuffed them out. (Opinion) God gave instruction regarding how things were to be done. (p. 47)

   "He, that being often reproved hardeneth his neck, shall suddenly be destroyed, and that without remedy" (Proverbs 29:1 KJV).

4. It burned to a crisp the bellyachers and gripers when they were gathered on the outskirts of the camp. (p. 48)

5. Two silver trumpets signaled the people to move with God. The camp stopped when God stopped. (p. 49) Silver trumpets called the congregation and directed the camp's movement. They signaled when it was time to come, and when it was time to go. (One trumpet called the leaders. Two trumpets called the congregation.) (p. 50)

6. God promised to save them from opponents—if they would sound the alarm—*before* confronting an enemy. For New Testament believers, this means to clap, sing, and shout praises to God (in addition to sounding a trumpet (or shofar?) *before* facing an enemy. (p. 52) Blessing the Lord, instead of bad–mouthing the enemy, brings victory.

7–10. (Opinion)

Study Guide/Journal for use with Why Shofars Wail in Scripture and Today—
The Exciting Stories and Miracles!   By Mary A. Bruno, Ph.D.

76

Chapter 9
Moving With God—Part 2

Date: _____

The shofar was mentioned on textbook pages: 53, 55, and 58.

Events or hurdles that you have faced while focusing on this chapter:

_____

_____

_____

_____

_____

_____

_____

_____

___True: ___False:

Prior to attempting this chapter, I have asked God to give me new wisdom and understanding and to reveal all that I need to learn or change at this time.

Study Guide/Journal for use with Why Shofars Wail in Scripture and Today—
The Exciting Stories and Miracles!   By Mary A. Bruno, Ph.D.

77

POINTS TO PONDER: (Sharing your answers in class is always optional.)

1. Main characters:

_____

_____

_____

_____

2. Key words:

_____

_____

_____

_____

3. Who or what carried the Ark of the Covenant (Testimony) and its furnishings on moving day?

_____

_____

4. (Four–part question) What was the four–step process (order) that was involved when preparing and moving the Ark of the Covenant?

_____

_____

Study Guide/Journal for use with Why Shofars Wail in Scripture and Today—
The Exciting Stories and Miracles!   By Mary A. Bruno, Ph.D.

78

_____

_____

_____

_____

_____

5. Upon what did the Ark's movers' survival depend?

_____

_____

6. God gave specific instructions to the Kohathites regarding when and how to transport the Ark. They were told to not to touch or peek at the holy things. Explain why God might tell someone, "No."

_____

_____

_____

7. (Two–part question) If God has ever warned you to go no further with a person, plan or thing, did you stop and obey Him or stay involved? Explain how that worked out for you.

_____

_____

_____

Study Guide/Journal for use with Why Shofars Wail in Scripture and Today—
The Exciting Stories and Miracles!   By Mary A. Bruno, Ph.D.

79

_____

_____

_____

_____

_____

_____

8. What size container could hold enough water to satisfy a thirsty camel?

_____

_____

9. Why were tribal banners (flags) important?

_____

_____

_____

10. Improve your communication skills by summarizing this chapter in twenty–five meaningful words or less.

_____

_____

_____

_____

_____

_____

Study Guide/Journal for use with Why Shofars Wail in Scripture and Today—
The Exciting Stories and Miracles!   By Mary A. Bruno, Ph.D.

80

Dear God, I love and appreciate You because:

_____

_____

_____

PRAYER REQUESTS/POTENTIAL MIRACLES:

"I will answer them before they even call to me.
While they are still talking about their needs,
I will go ahead and answer their prayers!"
(Isaiah 65:24 NLT)

_____

_____

_____

_____

_____

_____

_____

_____

_____

_____

_____

_____

_____

Study Guide/Journal for use with Why Shofars Wail in Scripture and Today—
The Exciting Stories and Miracles!　　　　By Mary A. Bruno, Ph.D.

_____

_____

_____

_____

_____

_____

_____

_____

NOTES:

God loves to inhabit His people's praises. To attract His attention, just sing, clap, shout, magnify His name, and, of course, release a few shofar blasts.

_____

_____

_____

Answers: Chapter 9

1–2. (Opinion)

3. The Kohathites (pp. 53–54)

4. The thick veil of the temple went on first, then the badger skin, the blue cloth, and golden poles (that were inserted into the rings). (pp. 53–54)

5. Their survival hinged on obedience (p. 54)

6. God wanted to save someone's life. (Opinion) (p. 54)

7. (Opinion)

8. The container would have to hold thirty–five–gallons, or more, which could equal 7–10, five–gallon buckets. (Opinion) (p. 54)

9. Flags gave direction and showed the tribes where they belonged. (p. 55)

10. (Opinion)

Study Guide/Journal for use with Why Shofars Wail in Scripture and Today—
The Exciting Stories and Miracles!   By Mary A. Bruno, Ph.D.

82

Chapter 10
Jubilee

Date_____

The shofar was mentioned on textbook pages: 59, 60, 61, 62, 63, and 64.

Events or hurdles that you have faced while focusing on this chapter:

_____

_____

_____

_____

_____

_____

_____

_____

___True: ___False:

Prior to attempting this chapter, I have asked God to give me new wisdom and understanding and to reveal all that I need to learn or change at this time.

Study Guide/Journal for use with Why Shofars Wail in Scripture and Today—
The Exciting Stories and Miracles!   By Mary A. Bruno, Ph.D.

POINTS TO PONDER: (Sharing your answers in class is always optional.)

1. Main characters:

_____

_____

_____

_____

2. Key words:

_____

_____

_____

_____

3. During what month(s) does the Day of Atonement (Yom Kippur) occur?

_____

_____

_____

_____

_____

_____

_____

Study Guide/Journal for use with Why Shofars Wail in Scripture and Today—
The Exciting Stories and Miracles!   By Mary A. Bruno, Ph.D.

84

4. (Two–part question) What kind of horn was the trumpet of the Jubilee? Please explain what kind of affect the sound of that horn had on those who were in bondage.

_____

_____

_____

_____

_____

_____

_____

5. What other types of blessings or invitations did the shofar calls convey?

_____

_____

_____

_____

_____

_____

_____

_____

_____

_____

Study Guide/Journal for use with Why Shofars Wail in Scripture and Today—
The Exciting Stories and Miracles!   By Mary A. Bruno, Ph.D.

85

6. Explain the impact that Jesus' divine breath and voice must have had upon the congregation when He stood in the synagogue and read Isaiah 61:1–2.

_____

_____

_____

_____

_____

_____

_____

7. According to Matthew 13:54–56 in the New Revised Standard Version Catholic Edition (NRSVCE) of the Holy Scriptures, how many children did the townspeople (who knew Mary and Joseph's family members—by name) indicate were in their family? Please write some of their children's names on the lines below. Consider what it must have been like to grow up in a family of that size and get to wear Jesus' hand-me-downs.

_____

_____

_____

_____

_____

_____

_____

_____

Study Guide/Journal for use with Why Shofars Wail in Scripture and Today—
The Exciting Stories and Miracles!   By Mary A. Bruno, Ph.D.

86

8. (Two–part question) What are your thoughts regarding God's Jubilee blessing (Leviticus 25:10) that is engraved on the United States of America's Liberty Bell? As we know, God honors His Word, which includes that passage on the Liberty Bell. We also know that the Liberty Bell's image was imprinted on a United States Postal Service's *Forever Stamp*. Consider or discuss what happens in the spiritual arena when that tiny postage stamp takes God's Word by land, by water, and by air—straight through the spiritual wickedness in high places—throughout the United States of America, its possessions, and on to distant lands.

_____

_____

_____

_____

_____

_____

_____

_____

_____

9. Please comment on your findings from this chapter.

_____

_____

_____

_____

Study Guide/Journal for use with Why Shofars Wail in Scripture and Today—
The Exciting Stories and Miracles!   By Mary A. Bruno, Ph.D.

87

_____

_____

_____

_____

_____

_____

_____

_____

10. Improve your communication skills by summarizing this chapter in twenty-five meaningful words or less.

_____

_____

_____

_____

_____

_____

Dear God, I love and appreciate You because:

_____

_____

_____

_____

Study Guide/Journal for use with Why Shofars Wail in Scripture and Today—
The Exciting Stories and Miracles! By Mary A. Bruno, Ph.D.

88

PRAYER REQUESTS/POTENTIAL MIRACLES:

"I will answer them before they even call to me.
While they are still talking about their needs,
I will go ahead and answer their prayers!"
(Isaiah 65:24 NLT)

_____

_____

_____

_____

_____

_____

_____

_____

_____

_____

_____

_____

_____

_____

_____

_____

_____

_____

*Study Guide/Journal for use with Why Shofars Wail in Scripture and Today—
The Exciting Stories and Miracles!*   By Mary A. Bruno, Ph.D.

_____

_____

_____

_____

_____

_____

_____

NOTES:

_____

_____

_____

_____

Answers: Chapter 10

1–2. (Opinion)

3. The Day of Atonement is on the 10th day of the 7th month (Tishri) on the Jewish calendar, which is in late September or early October. (p. 59)

4. The trumpet of the jubilee was a shofar that released a joyful message. (p. 59)

5. It announced freedom and brought powerful flashes of hope, and thanksgiving to God. Jubilee shofars called to come closer to God, to enter His Presence, to hear His voice, to receive His love and gifts, to let God heal hurts and make life better. They called to put away idols, to repent of all that was not pleasing to God, to sever all fellowship with sin, to enter into God's rest, refreshing, and favor, and to saturate in His love. (p.60)

6. Jesus' voice must have had shofar impact. (p. 61)

7. People of their town knew that Mary and Joseph had, at least, seven children. Joseph fathered all but the first one of them (Jesus). (p. 62)

8–10. (Opinion)

Study Guide/Journal for use with Why Shofars Wail in Scripture and Today—
The Exciting Stories and Miracles!   By Mary A. Bruno, Ph.D.

90

Chapter 11
Jericho—Part 1: Groomed

Date: _____

The shofar was mentioned on textbook pages: 69 and 72.

Events or hurdles that you have faced while focusing on this chapter:

_____

_____

_____

_____

_____

_____

_____

_____

___True: ___False:

Prior to attempting this chapter, I have asked God to give me new wisdom and understanding and to reveal all that I need to learn or change at this time.

Study Guide/Journal for use with Why Shofars Wail in Scripture and Today—
The Exciting Stories and Miracles!   By Mary A. Bruno, Ph.D.

91

POINTS TO PONDER: (Sharing your answers in class is always optional.)

1. Main characters:

_____

_____

_____

_____

2. Key words:

_____

_____

_____

_____

3. What kind of influence and impact, did Moses have on Joshua's life?

_____

_____

_____

_____

_____

_____

_____

_____

_____

Study Guide/Journal for use with Why Shofars Wail in Scripture and Today—
The Exciting Stories and Miracles!   By Mary A. Bruno, Ph.D.

92

4. (Two-part question) Upon what did Moses rest as Aaron and Hur raised his hands toward heaven? Explain if that source of rest reminds you of anything similar that brings rest to believers during their times of spiritual battle. [Hint] *Ha Tsur*— (Ex 17:6; Deut 32:4, 15, 18, 30, 31; Isa. 17:10; 26:10; 32:12; 51:1; Ps. 19:14; and 1 Cor. 10:4.)

---

5. (Two-part question) Why would anyone ask God to *discomfit* an enemy? Please tell of when God may have discomfited your enemy/enemies.

Study Guide/Journal for use with Why Shofars Wail in Scripture and Today—
The Exciting Stories and Miracles!   By Mary A. Bruno, Ph.D.

6. (Two-part question) In what battle did Jehovah Nissi's unseen Presence become Joshua's, real Victory Banner? Please discuss if or when God has ever fought any of your battles.

_____

_____

_____

_____

_____

_____

_____

_____

_____

7. How did God interrupt the stoning of His servant?

_____

_____

_____

_____

_____

8. (Four-part question) Given the risk of stoning, how might you have handled Joshua's anointing for leadership? How did God tell Moses to get it

Study Guide/Journal for use with Why Shofars Wail in Scripture and Today—
The Exciting Stories and Miracles!   By Mary A. Bruno, Ph.D.

94

done? In addition to the anointing, what else was involved when Moses transferred his command to Joshua? How do you suppose Moses died?

_____

_____

_____

_____

_____

_____

_____

_____

_____

_____

_____

9. (Three–part question) Is God's voice calling as an inner shofar for you to come up higher and closer to Him? What additional biblical passages, examples, memories, or questions, came to mind while reading this chapter? How did they relate to your life or things that need to continue or change?

_____

_____

_____

_____

_____

Study Guide/Journal for use with Why Shofars Wail in Scripture and Today—
The Exciting Stories and Miracles!   By Mary A. Bruno, Ph.D.

95

_____

_____

_____

_____

_____

_____

_____

10. Improve your communication skills by summarizing this chapter in twenty–five meaningful words or less.

_____

_____

_____

_____

_____

_____

_____

Dear God, I love and appreciate You because:

_____

_____

_____

_____

Study Guide/Journal for use with Why Shofars Wail in Scripture and Today—
The Exciting Stories and Miracles!   By Mary A. Bruno, Ph.D.

96

PRAYER REQUESTS/POTENTIAL MIRACLES:

"I will answer them before they even call to me.
While they are still talking about their needs,
I will go ahead and answer their prayers!"
(Isaiah 65:24 NLT)

_____

_____

_____

_____

_____

_____

_____

_____

_____

_____

_____

_____

_____

_____

_____

_____

*Study Guide/Journal for use with Why Shofars Wail in Scripture and Today—
The Exciting Stories and Miracles!*　　　　　By Mary A. Bruno, Ph.D.

_____

_____

_____

_____

_____

_____

NOTES:

_____

_____

_____

_____

Answers: Chapter 11

1–2. (Opinion)

3. The two of them were very close. Numbers 11:28 and Exodus 24:13 confirm that Joshua was Moses' assistant. (pp. 65–66)

4. It was a rock (p. 66) (Opinion) See 1 Corinthians 10:1–4.

5. *Discomfit* meant to weaken the enemy's power. (Opinion) (p. 67)

6. God was Joshua's unseen Victory Banner in the battle against Amalek. (p. 68) (See Exodus 17:9–16)

7. When God manifested His glory in the tabernacle, everyone had to rush to the place of worship—even if they had to interrupt the stoning (killing) of His anointed servant(s). (p. 69)

8. (Opinion) God told Moses to assemble everyone and to inaugurate Joshua as the new leader. Moses laid his hands on him and transferred some of his authority to Joshua. (pp. 69–70)

9–10. (Opinion)

Study Guide/Journal for use with Why Shofars Wail in Scripture and Today—
The Exciting Stories and Miracles!   By Mary A. Bruno, Ph.D.

98

Chapter 12
Jericho—Part 2: Preliminaries

Date: _____

The shofar was mentioned on textbook page: 78.

Events or hurdles that you have faced while focusing on this chapter:

_____

_____

_____

_____

_____

_____

_____

_____

___True: ___False:

Prior to attempting this chapter, I have asked God to give me new wisdom and understanding and to reveal all that I need to learn or change at this time.

Study Guide/Journal for use with Why Shofars Wail in Scripture and Today—
The Exciting Stories and Miracles!　　　　　By Mary A. Bruno, Ph.D.

POINTS TO PONDER: (Sharing your answers in class is always optional.)

1. Main characters:

_____

_____

_____

_____

2. Key words:

_____

_____

_____

_____

3. Discuss what was happening in the supernatural arena when God told Joshua to, "Be strong and of good courage."

_____

_____

_____

_____

_____

_____

_____

Study Guide/Journal for use with Why Shofars Wail in Scripture and Today—
The Exciting Stories and Miracles!   By Mary A. Bruno, Ph.D.

100

4. Summarize the meaning of *receive* (*lambano)* that Jesus used in Acts 1:8.

_____

_____

_____

_____

_____

_____

_____

5. (Two-part question) Review the meanings of the words *power* and *virtue,* and then discuss what Jesus must have experienced when He felt "virtue" go out of Him in Mark 5:30. Is there a difference between *power* and *virtue?*

_____

_____

_____

_____

_____

_____

_____

_____

_____

_____

Study Guide/Journal for use with Why Shofars Wail in Scripture and Today—
The Exciting Stories and Miracles!   By Mary A. Bruno, Ph.D.

101

6. (Five–part question) Why was it important for Joshua to reinstitute the rite of circumcision—before his shofar sounding victory? Has God ever urged you to cut off a habit, relationship, etc., that hindered you from receiving His blessings? If so, what happened, and how long did it take to end it? Did God bring something better into your life afterward? Please explain.

_____

_____

_____

_____

_____

_____

_____

_____

_____

_____

_____

_____

_____

_____

_____

_____

_____

_____

_____

Study Guide/Journal for use with Why Shofars Wail in Scripture and Today—
The Exciting Stories and Miracles!   By Mary A. Bruno, Ph.D.

102

7. (Two–part question) Is there anything in your life that hinders your walk with God? If so, are you ready to tell God about it and receive His power and grace to end it *today*, and make room for His greater blessings? (Since this is a personal matter between you and the Lord, it is okay to write in "code.")

_____

_____

_____

_____

_____

_____

_____

_____

8. Discuss other biblical passages, examples, or memories that came to mind while studying this chapter, and what action(s) God may want you to take regarding them.

_____

_____

_____

_____

_____

_____

_____

Study Guide/Journal for use with Why Shofars Wail in Scripture and Today—
The Exciting Stories and Miracles!   By Mary A. Bruno, Ph.D.

103

_____

_____

9. Lessons learned or special insights about the Lord and His loving involvement with His people.

_____

_____

_____

_____

_____

_____

_____

_____

_____

10. Improve your communication skills by summarizing this chapter in twenty–five meaningful words or less.

_____

_____

_____

_____

_____

_____

Study Guide/Journal for use with Why Shofars Wail in Scripture and Today—
The Exciting Stories and Miracles!　　　　By Mary A. Bruno, Ph.D.

104

Dear God, I love and appreciate You because:

_____

_____

_____

PRAYER REQUESTS/POTENTIAL MIRACLES:

"I will answer them before they even call to me.
While they are still talking about their needs,
I will go ahead and answer their prayers!"
(Isaiah 65:24 NLT)

_____

_____

_____

_____

_____

_____

_____

_____

_____

_____

_____

_____

_____

_____

Study Guide/Journal for use with Why Shofars Wail in Scripture and Today—
The Exciting Stories and Miracles!   By Mary A. Bruno, Ph.D.

105

_____

_____

_____

_____

_____

_____

_____

_____

_____

_____

_____

NOTES:

_____

_____

_____

_____

Answers: Chapter 12

1–2. (Opinion)

3. God was imparting His strength to Joshua. (p. 73)

4. *Lambano* means to lay hold of, or take in order to carry away, etc. (p. 77)

5. (Opinion) There is no difference between *power* and *virtue*. (pp. 76–77)

6. The men had to be circumcised before they could claim (qualify for) God's covenant promise. (p. 78) (Opinion)

7–10. (Opinion)

Study Guide/Journal for use with Why Shofars Wail in Scripture and Today—
The Exciting Stories and Miracles!   By Mary A. Bruno, Ph.D.

106

Chapter 13
Jericho—Part 3: Holy Ground

Date: _____

The shofar was mentioned on textbook pages: 82 and 83,

Events or hurdles that you have faced while focusing on this chapter:

_____

_____

_____

_____

_____

_____

_____

_____

_____

_____

___True: ___False:

Prior to attempting this chapter, I have asked God to give me new wisdom and understanding and to reveal all that I need to learn or change at this time.

Study Guide/Journal for use with Why Shofars Wail in Scripture and Today—
The Exciting Stories and Miracles!   By Mary A. Bruno, Ph.D.

107

POINTS TO PONDER: (Sharing your answers in class is always optional.)

1. Main characters:

_____

_____

_____

_____

2. Key words:

_____

_____

_____

_____

3. (Three–part question) What did God give Moses to go with his new calling and new commission? What can you expect from God when He gives you a new assignment or area of responsibility? Explain if you have experienced anything similar from God.

_____

_____

_____

_____

_____

_____

Study Guide/Journal for use with Why Shofars Wail in Scripture and Today—
The Exciting Stories and Miracles!   By Mary A. Bruno, Ph.D.

108

_____

_____

_____

_____

_____

_____

_____

_____

_____

_____

_____

4. (Two–part question) God, being full of surprises, also gave Moses a two–part sign. Please explain what the sign was, and if it came to pass.

_____

_____

_____

_____

_____

_____

_____

_____

_____

Study Guide/Journal for use with Why Shofars Wail in Scripture and Today—
The Exciting Stories and Miracles! By Mary A. Bruno, Ph.D.

109

5. Why was Joshua happy when the Commander of the Lord's army told him to remove his sandal?

_____

_____

_____

_____

_____

_____

6. (Three–part question) Name some important details regarding the daily lineup, including shofars, and Rahab's family's responsibilities during the Jericho victory. Has God ever led you to keep silent about anything that He was working on? If so, please explain.

_____

_____

_____

_____

_____

_____

_____

_____

_____

_____

_____

_____

_____

Study Guide/Journal for use with Why Shofars Wail in Scripture and Today—
The Exciting Stories and Miracles!   By Mary A. Bruno, Ph.D.

110

_____

_____

_____

7. What kind of men were inside Jericho's walls?

_____

_____

_____

_____

_____

_____

8. (Two–part question) Name two of Rahab's famous descendants. Why do you think God included her name in both of His Testaments?

_____

_____

_____

_____

_____

_____

_____

_____

_____

_____

Study Guide/Journal for use with Why Shofars Wail in Scripture and Today—
The Exciting Stories and Miracles!   By Mary A. Bruno, Ph.D.

111

9. Lessons learned, and insights or comments regarding this chapter.

_____

_____

_____

_____

_____

_____

_____

10. Improve your communication skills by summarizing this chapter in twenty–five meaningful words or less.

_____

_____

_____

_____

_____

_____

Dear God, I love and appreciate You because:

_____

_____

_____

Study Guide/Journal for use with Why Shofars Wail in Scripture and Today—
The Exciting Stories and Miracles! By Mary A. Bruno, Ph.D.

112

PRAYER REQUESTS/POTENTIAL MIRACLES:

"I will answer them before they even call to me.
While they are still talking about their needs,
I will go ahead and answer their prayers!"
(Isaiah 65:24 NLT)

_____

_____

_____

_____

_____

_____

_____

_____

_____

_____

_____

_____

_____

_____

_____

_____

_____

_____

_____

Study Guide/Journal for use with Why Shofars Wail in Scripture and Today—
The Exciting Stories and Miracles!   By Mary A. Bruno, Ph.D.

_____

_____

_____

_____

NOTES:

_____

_____

_____

Answers: Chapter 13

1–2. (Opinion)

3. God gave Moses a new anointing to lead God's flock, plus His miraculous equipping power, with God-given position, God-given authority, and God-given miracles. (pp. 79–80)

4. Part 1: God told Moses that He would be with him. Part 2: when Moses brought the people out of Egypt, he would worship God again on that mountain. (p. 80)

5. Joshua knew that something good was coming from God. (Whenever God asks you to lay something aside, it is probably because He wants make room in your life so that He can give you something that you will like much better.) (p. 81)

6. One scarlet cord, seven shofars, the Ark of the Covenant, quiet times, the line-up, marching, and lots of shouting at the right time and in the right place. Rahab's family had to stay in her house and not tell anyone about the spies' mission. (Opinion) (pp. 82–83)

7. The men of Jericho were experienced fighting men. (p. 82)

8. Two of Rahab's famous descendants include Boaz and Jesus. (Opinion) God may have memorialized Rahab's name in His Book because she was a courageous woman of faith, and, as we know, faith (believing what God says) always attracts His Presence. (p. 84)

9–10. (Opinion)

Study Guide/Journal for use with Why Shofars Wail in Scripture and Today—
The Exciting Stories and Miracles!   By Mary A. Bruno, Ph.D.

114

Chapter 14
Jericho—Part 4: The Blasts

Date: _____

The shofar was mentioned on textbook pages: 85, 86, 87, 88, 90, 91, and 92.

Events or hurdles that you have faced while focusing on this chapter:

_____

_____

_____

_____

_____

_____

_____

_____

___True: ___False:

Prior to attempting this chapter, I have asked God to give me new wisdom and understanding and to reveal all that I need to learn or change at this time.

Study Guide/Journal for use with Why Shofars Wail in Scripture and Today—
The Exciting Stories and Miracles!   By Mary A. Bruno, Ph.D.

115

POINTS TO PONDER: (Sharing your answers in class is always optional.)

1. Main characters:

_____

_____

_____

_____

2. Key words:

_____

_____

_____

_____

3. (Three–part question) Have you ever lost your voice or had to go for a week without speaking to anyone? If so, what were some of your frustrations? How do you think Joshua's men coped with their gag order?

_____

_____

_____

_____

_____

_____

_____

Study Guide/Journal for use with Why Shofars Wail in Scripture and Today—
The Exciting Stories and Miracles!   By Mary A. Bruno, Ph.D.

116

_____

_____

_____

4. (Two–part question) Comment on what it must have been like for Joshua's fighting men to march in silence as the priest's shofars sent God's wordless message. As the men paraded daily around Jericho they may have been on the receiving end of taunts, jeers, and ridicule from people behind the walls. What do you suppose Joshua's warriors may have thought, felt, or planned?

_____

_____

_____

_____

_____

_____

5. The Ark of the Covenant was a treasured object. Why do you think God included it in the marching order?

_____

_____

_____

_____

_____

_____

Study Guide/Journal for use with Why Shofars Wail in Scripture and Today—
The Exciting Stories and Miracles!   By Mary A. Bruno, Ph.D.

117

6. What kinds of trumpets were mentioned in Joshua 6:12–14?

_____

_____

_____

_____

7. (Three–part question) What, if anything, may have been different on days, two, three, and four, or on days five and six of the march around Jericho? How strong do you think the marchers' faith was on days 1–3? How well do you think their faith was holding up on days 4–6?

_____

_____

_____

_____

_____

_____

_____

_____

_____

_____

_____

8. (Two–part question) When it was time to shout, what kind of message do you think Joshua's unsilenced men shouted to the Lord and possibly to the

Study Guide/Journal for use with Why Shofars Wail in Scripture and Today—
The Exciting Stories and Miracles!   By Mary A. Bruno, Ph.D.

118

Jerichonians? What happened to Rahab's house that was in/on the wall during Jericho's crumbling defeat?

_____

_____

_____

_____

_____

_____

_____

9. Lessons learned or special insights about the Lord and His loving involvement with His people.

_____

_____

_____

_____

_____

_____

_____

_____

_____

Study Guide/Journal for use with Why Shofars Wail in Scripture and Today—
The Exciting Stories and Miracles!   By Mary A. Bruno, Ph.D.

_____

_____

_____

_____

_____

_____

_____

_____

10. Improve your communication skills by summarizing this chapter in twenty–five meaningful words or less.

_____

_____

_____

_____

_____

_____

Dear God, I love and appreciate You because:

_____

_____

_____

_____

Study Guide/Journal for use with Why Shofars Wail in Scripture and Today—
The Exciting Stories and Miracles!   By Mary A. Bruno, Ph.D.

120

PRAYER REQUESTS/POTENTIAL MIRACLES:

"I will answer them before they even call to me.
While they are still talking about their needs,
I will go ahead and answer their prayers!"
(Isaiah 65:24 NLT)

_____

_____

_____

_____

_____

_____

_____

_____

_____

_____

_____

_____

_____

_____

_____

_____

_____

_____

Study Guide/Journal for use with Why Shofars Wail in Scripture and Today—
The Exciting Stories and Miracles!   By Mary A. Bruno, Ph.D.

_____

_____

_____

_____

_____

_____

_____

_____

NOTES:

_____

_____

_____

_____

_____

_____

Answers: Chapter 14

1–4. (Opinion)

5. (Opinion) God may have included the Ark in their daily marches to give the people a visual reminder that He was with them. (p. 85)

6. The trumpets were rams' horns—shofars. (p. 86)

7. (Speculation/Opinion)

8. (Opinion) Disaster was all around Rahab and her family, but her home stood tall and strong as a tower of faith, through Jericho's disaster. (p. 90)

9–10. (Opinion)

Study Guide/Journal for use with Why Shofars Wail in Scripture and Today—
The Exciting Stories and Miracles! By Mary A. Bruno, Ph.D.

122

Chapter 15
Daring Deliverance

Date: _____

The shofar was mentioned on textbook pages: 95, 97, and 98.

Events or hurdles that you have faced while focusing on this chapter:

_____

_____

_____

_____

_____

_____

_____

_____

_____

___True: ___False:

Prior to attempting this chapter, I have asked God to give me new wisdom and understanding and to reveal all that I need to learn or change at this time.

Study Guide/Journal for use with Why Shofars Wail in Scripture and Today—
The Exciting Stories and Miracles!   By Mary A. Bruno, Ph.D.

123

POINTS TO PONDER: (Sharing your answers in class is always optional.)

1. Main characters:

_____

_____

_____

_____

2. Key words:

_____

_____

_____

_____

3. (Two–part question) Why did God leave some ungodly nations in Judges 3:1–2? Can you give an example of how His reason for doing so may apply in your life?

_____

_____

_____

_____

_____

_____

_____

Study Guide/Journal for use with Why Shofars Wail in Scripture and Today—
The Exciting Stories and Miracles!   By Mary A. Bruno, Ph.D.

124

_____

_____

4. (Two–part question) What did the Israelites do that caused problems in their relationship with God and led to years of bondage and misery? What would you tell a believer who was considering that kind of decision?

_____

_____

_____

_____

_____

_____

5. (Two–part question) Why is the way of transgressors so hard? What happened to the Jericho prize that Israel had won by obedience?

_____

_____

_____

_____

_____

_____

_____

_____

_____

Study Guide/Journal for use with Why Shofars Wail in Scripture and Today—
The Exciting Stories and Miracles!   By Mary A. Bruno, Ph.D.

125

6. (Three–part question) When did God raise up someone to help His people? Has God ever sent anyone to help you during an important time of decision? Please explain.

_____

_____

_____

_____

_____

_____

_____

_____

_____

_____

7. (Two-part question) Do you believe God's promise in 2 Chronicles 7:13–14 is for us today? How do His "Ifs" affect the results of our decisions?

_____

_____

_____

_____

_____

_____

Study Guide/Journal for use with Why Shofars Wail in Scripture and Today—
The Exciting Stories and Miracles!   By Mary A. Bruno, Ph.D.

126

_____

_____

_____

8. (Four–part question) After wielding his homemade sword, what did Ehud do that drew God's soldiers to rise up, line up, and follow up? After the enemy was defeated, what else did Ehud do? Are there any enemy inroads in your life that God wants you to address? Explain.

_____

_____

_____

_____

_____

_____

_____

_____

_____

_____

_____

_____

_____

_____

_____

_____

Study Guide/Journal for use with Why Shofars Wail in Scripture and Today—
The Exciting Stories and Miracles! By Mary A. Bruno, Ph.D.

127

9. What lessons or special insights have you learned about the Lord and His loving involvement with His people?

_____

_____

_____

_____

_____

_____

_____

_____

_____

_____

_____

10. Improve your communication skills by summarizing this chapter in twenty–five meaningful words or less.

_____

_____

_____

_____

_____

Study Guide/Journal for use with Why Shofars Wail in Scripture and Today—
The Exciting Stories and Miracles!　　　　　By Mary A. Bruno, Ph.D.

128

Dear God, I love and appreciate You because:

_____

_____

_____

PRAYER REQUESTS/POTENTIAL MIRACLES:

"I will answer them before they even call to me.
While they are still talking about their needs,
I will go ahead and answer their prayers!"
(Isaiah 65:24 NLT)

_____

_____

_____

_____

_____

_____

_____

_____

_____

_____

_____

_____

_____

_____

Study Guide/Journal for use with Why Shofars Wail in Scripture and Today—
The Exciting Stories and Miracles!   By Mary A. Bruno, Ph.D.

129

_____

_____

_____

_____

_____

_____

NOTES:

_____

_____

_____

Answers: Chapter 15

1–2. (Opinion)

3. God left a few ungodly nations around so that the Israelites could learn to war (Could use them for sparring partners and target practice). (Opinion) (p. 93)

4. They married unbelievers. (Opinion) (p. 93)

5. The transgressors' ways were hard so they would wise up, repent, return to God, and receive His blessings. The Jericho prize was lost because of Israel's disobedience. (p. 94)

6. When the people prayed—God sent someone (Ehud) to help them. (Opinion) (p. 94)

7. God promised that if His people would humble themselves and pray, and turn from their wicked ways, He would forgive their sin and heal their land. (Opinion) (p. 95)

8. Ehud blew his shofar that compelled God's soldiers to rise up, line up, and follow up. They defeated the enemy, and then closed off his crossing places (areas of access). (pp. 97–98) (Opinion)

9–10. (Opinion)

Study Guide/Journal for use with Why Shofars Wail in Scripture and Today—
The Exciting Stories and Miracles!   By Mary A. Bruno, Ph.D.

130

Chapter 16
Gideon's Preparation

Date: _____

The shofar was mentioned on textbook pages: 99 and 107.

Events or hurdles that you have faced while focusing on this chapter:

_____
_____
_____
_____
_____
_____
_____
_____
_____

___True: ___False:

Prior to attempting this chapter, I have asked God to give me new wisdom and understanding and to reveal all that I need to learn or change at this time.

Study Guide/Journal for use with Why Shofars Wail in Scripture and Today—
The Exciting Stories and Miracles!   By Mary A. Bruno, Ph.D.

POINTS TO PONDER: (Sharing your answers in class is always optional.)

1. Main characters:

_____

_____

_____

_____

2. Key words:

_____

_____

_____

_____

3. (Two–part question) After seven years of poverty and misery under merciless tyrants, what happened that brought change and good things? Why do you suppose it took so long?

_____

_____

_____

_____

_____

_____

_____

Study Guide/Journal for use with Why Shofars Wail in Scripture and Today—
The Exciting Stories and Miracles!   By Mary A. Bruno, Ph.D.

132

4. (Three–part question) When God gave Gideon strength, what did Gideon give God? Share about when you may have done something similar. How did that work out?

_____

_____

_____

_____

_____

_____

_____

_____

_____

_____

5. How did Gideon live up to the meaning of his name?

_____

_____

_____

_____

_____

_____

_____

_____

Study Guide/Journal for use with Why Shofars Wail in Scripture and Today—
The Exciting Stories and Miracles!   By Mary A. Bruno, Ph.D.

133

_____

_____

_____

6. (Five–part question) What kind of strength did God give Gideon? With what did God clothe Gideon? How would you feel if you had to face an enemy while clothed in like manner? Have you ever experienced a new or special covering from God? Explain.

_____

_____

_____

_____

_____

_____

_____

_____

_____

_____

7. (Four–part question) What was a sure sign that Gideon had been in God's Presence? Have you ever experienced that kind of sign? Explain. How did Gideon's offerings change as he continued to walk with God?

_____

_____

Study Guide/Journal for use with Why Shofars Wail in Scripture and Today—
The Exciting Stories and Miracles!   By Mary A. Bruno, Ph.D.

134

_____

_____

_____

_____

_____

_____

_____

8. (Three–part question) Why was it important for Gideon to pull down his father's idol altar? Has God ever asked you to do anything similar? Explain.

_____

_____

_____

_____

_____

_____

_____

_____

_____

_____

_____

_____

_____

Study Guide/Journal for use with Why Shofars Wail in Scripture and Today—
The Exciting Stories and Miracles! By Mary A. Bruno, Ph.D.

135

_____

_____

_____

9. By God's grace I will address and/or change the following, to make more room for God's Presence and plans in my life:

_____

_____

_____

_____

_____

_____

_____

_____

10. Improve your communication skills by summarizing this chapter in twenty–five meaningful words or less.

_____

_____

_____

_____

_____

_____

_____

_____

Study Guide/Journal for use with Why Shofars Wail in Scripture and Today—
The Exciting Stories and Miracles!   By Mary A. Bruno, Ph.D.

136

Dear God, I love and appreciate You because:

_____

_____

_____

_____

PRAYER REQUESTS/POTENTIAL MIRACLES:

"I will answer them before they even call to me.
While they are still talking about their needs,
I will go ahead and answer their prayers!"
(Isaiah 65:24 NLT)

_____

_____

_____

_____

_____

_____

_____

_____

_____

_____

_____

_____

Study Guide/Journal for use with Why Shofars Wail in Scripture and Today—
The Exciting Stories and Miracles!   By Mary A. Bruno, Ph.D.

137

_____

_____

_____

_____

_____

_____

_____

_____

NOTES:

_____

_____

_____

Answers: Chapter 16

1–2. (Opinion)

3. When the *men* prayed, God heard, answered, and sent someone (Gideon) to help them. (Opinion) (p. 99)

4. Gideon gave God excuses. (Opinion) (p. 100)

5. Gideon's name meant, *hewer*, one who could cut and gather, as to gather, to cut wood, and to carve. God used him to gather and carve out a victorious shofar-blowing army for Israel. (pp. 101–102).

6. The strength that God gave Gideon was God's strength. God clothed Gideon with Himself. (Opinions) (p. 102) (See Judges 6:34 AMP, p. 109 in chapter 17.)

7. One sure sign of having been with God was a burning desire to give to God. (Opinion) (p. 102) Gideon's offerings increased greatly in size. (p. 105)

8. Joash's idol altar was a spiritual stronghold that did not honor God. (Opinion) (pp. 105–106)

9–10. (Opinion)

Study Guide/Journal for use with Why Shofars Wail in Scripture and Today—
The Exciting Stories and Miracles!   By Mary A. Bruno, Ph.D.

138

Chapter 17
Gideon's Shofars

Date: _____

The shofar was mentioned on textbook pages: 109, 110, 112, 113, 114, 115, and 116.

Events or hurdles that you have faced while focusing on this chapter:

_____

_____

_____

_____

_____

_____

_____

_____

___True: ___False:

Prior to attempting this chapter, I have asked God to give me new wisdom and understanding and to reveal all that I need to learn or change at this time.

Study Guide/Journal for use with Why Shofars Wail in Scripture and Today—
The Exciting Stories and Miracles!   By Mary A. Bruno, Ph.D.

139

POINTS TO PONDER: (Sharing your answers in class is always optional.)

1. Main characters:

_____

_____

_____

_____

2. Key words:

_____

_____

_____

_____

3. (Two–part question) What changed for Gideon after God's Spirit embraced (clothed) him? How many fighting men answered Gideon's shofar call?

_____

_____

_____

_____

_____

_____

_____

_____

Study Guide/Journal for use with Why Shofars Wail in Scripture and Today—
The Exciting Stories and Miracles!   By Mary A. Bruno, Ph.D.

140

4. How did Gideon's response to having heard the Midianite's dream, reveal his remarkable character?

_____

_____

_____

_____

_____

_____

_____

5. What were Gideon's men's weapons of warfare? How did they compare to 2 Corinthians 10:3–5 and Ephesians 6:17?

_____

_____

_____

_____

_____

_____

_____

_____

_____

_____

Study Guide/Journal for use with Why Shofars Wail in Scripture and Today—
The Exciting Stories and Miracles!　　　　　　By Mary A. Bruno, Ph.D.

141

6. (Five-part question) What were the trumpets in Judges 7:18? Have you ever blown one? Explain. If not, would you like to? Why?

_____

_____

_____

_____

_____

_____

_____

_____

_____

_____

7. (Two-part question) How could the enemy armies have overestimated the size of Gideon's army? When they heard the blaring shofars, in which direction did they turn their attack?

_____

_____

_____

_____

_____

_____

Study Guide/Journal for use with Why Shofars Wail in Scripture and Today—
The Exciting Stories and Miracles!   By Mary A. Bruno, Ph.D.

142

_____

_____

_____

_____

8. (Three–part question) Of what may Gideon have been reminded as he observed Oreb and Zeeb's dangling heads? Is the Lord reminding you of victories that He has helped you to win? Please explain.

_____

_____

_____

_____

_____

_____

_____

_____

_____

_____

_____

_____

_____

Study Guide/Journal for use with Why Shofars Wail in Scripture and Today—
The Exciting Stories and Miracles!   By Mary A. Bruno, Ph.D.

143

9. Lessons learned, and insights or comments regarding this chapter.

_____

_____

_____

_____

_____

_____

10. Challenge yourself and polish your communication skills by summarizing this chapter in twenty–five meaningful words or less.

_____

_____

_____

_____

_____

_____

_____

Dear God, I love and appreciate You because:

_____

_____

_____

_____

Study Guide/Journal for use with Why Shofars Wail in Scripture and Today—
The Exciting Stories and Miracles!   By Mary A. Bruno, Ph.D.

144

PRAYER REQUESTS/POTENTIAL MIRACLES:

"I will answer them before they even call to me.
While they are still talking about their needs,
I will go ahead and answer their prayers!"
(Isaiah 65:24 NLT)

_____

_____

_____

_____

_____

_____

_____

_____

_____

_____

_____

_____

_____

_____

_____

_____

_____

_____

Study Guide/Journal for use with Why Shofars Wail in Scripture and Today—
The Exciting Stories and Miracles!   By Mary A. Bruno, Ph.D.

_____

_____

_____

_____

_____

_____

_____

NOTES:

_____

_____

_____

Answers: Chapter 17

1–2. (Opinion)

3. Soldiers recognized Gideon's leadership and stood at attention when he spoke. (p. 109) Thirty–two–thousand (32,000) warriors answered Gideon's call. (p. 110)

4. Instead of running to tell his men that God had given victory, Gideon took time to humbly bow and worship the Lord. (p. 111)

5. Their weapons were not fleshly, but spiritual, and powerful through God. (p. 112)

6. Those trumpets were *shofars.* (Opinions) (pp. 112–113)

7. The enemy's leaders may have thought that each of the shofar blasts represented another commander with another 100 men. The enemy army turned the attack inward and self-destructed. (p. 114)

8. The *rock of Oreb* and *winepress of Zeeb* may have reminded Gideon of the rock where he had met with God, and of the winepress where he had ground wheat to hide it from Zeeb. (pp. 115–116)

9–10. (Opinion)

Study Guide/Journal for use with Why Shofars Wail in Scripture and Today—
The Exciting Stories and Miracles!　　　　　　By Mary A. Bruno, Ph.D.

146

Chapter 18
King Saul Blew It!

Date: _____

The shofar was mentioned on textbook pages: 117, 118, and 122.

Events or hurdles that you have faced while focusing on this chapter:

_____

_____

_____

_____

_____

_____

_____

_____

___True: ___False:

Prior to attempting this chapter, I have asked God to give me new wisdom and understanding and to reveal all that I need to learn or change at this time.

Study Guide/Journal for use with Why Shofars Wail in Scripture and Today—
The Exciting Stories and Miracles!   By Mary A. Bruno, Ph.D.

POINTS TO PONDER: (Sharing your answers in class is always optional.)

1. Main characters:

_____

_____

_____

_____

2. Key words:

_____

_____

_____

_____

3. Comment on the differences and results between Gideon's anointed shofar blasts, and King Saul's fleshly shofar wails.

_____

_____

_____

_____

_____

_____

_____

_____

Study Guide/Journal for use with Why Shofars Wail in Scripture and Today—
The Exciting Stories and Miracles!   By Mary A. Bruno, Ph.D.

148

4. (Two–part question) Comment on what can we learn from when Saul grew tired of waiting for Samuel, usurped Samuel's authority, and took it upon himself to offer a burnt offering. What was Saul's penalty for his arrogant and disrespectful action?

_____

_____

_____

_____

_____

_____

_____

_____

5. How did Saul attempt to satisfy his craving for spiritual guidance after God's voice went silent?

_____

_____

_____

_____

_____

6. Saul's experience with alternative counsel was exciting for the moment, but how did that work out for him, his family members, and his army?

_____

_____

Study Guide/Journal for use with Why Shofars Wail in Scripture and Today—
The Exciting Stories and Miracles!   By Mary A. Bruno, Ph.D.

149

_____

_____

_____

7. After reading about what happened with King Saul, you may have realized that experimenting with counterfeits of God's counsel, such as: the Occult: psychics, fortunetellers, horoscopes, or Ouija boards, tarot cards, palm readers, tea leaf readers, spiritualists, divination, magic, witchcraft (including the reading of books about witchcraft and watching TV programs or movies about witchcraft), etc., could be spiritually harmful to you or your loved ones. Many have consulted counterfeit counsel or false religions and afterward have noticed dark shadowy spirit figures hoovering near them and moving throughout their homes.

If that has happened to you, it is time to exercise your authority in Jesus' name, and command them to leave. If you have experimented with any of the above, it is very important to renounce it, turn from it, ask God's forgiveness, and then—Do not give the books, etc., away!—burn all of the ungodly materials. You may pause right here and right now and renounce any and all of the above involvement. The following sample prayer may help.

Prayer to forsake ungodly involvement or false religion:

Dear Lord God Most High,

I confess that I have cheated on you and committed spiritual adultery, when I sought after or relied on guidance from evil workers of spiritual darkness, instead of being content to rely in You and Your Holy Word.

I reject and forsake all involvement with evil, ungodly counsel, witchcraft, and counterfeit religion. Please forgive me, cleanse me, and fill me with Your Holy Presence. By the authority of Jesus' name, I order all dark spirits and powers to leave me now.

Thank You, Lord God, for making me free. Please teach me to walk in Your ways and led me by Your Holy Spirit and Your Word. In Jesus' name, I pray. Amen. (It is okay to offer Father God a hug.)

Study Guide/Journal for use with Why Shofars Wail in Scripture and Today—
The Exciting Stories and Miracles!   By Mary A. Bruno, Ph.D.

150

P.S: _____

_____

_____

_____

_____

_____

8. Lessons learned or special insights about the Lord and His loving involvement with His people.

_____

_____

_____

_____

_____

_____

_____

_____

_____

_____

_____

9. By God's grace, I will address and/or change the following, to make more room for His Presence and plans in my life.

_____

_____

Study Guide/Journal for use with Why Shofars Wail in Scripture and Today—
The Exciting Stories and Miracles!   By Mary A. Bruno, Ph.D.

151

_____

_____

_____

_____

_____

_____

_____

_____

10. Improve your communication skills by summarizing this chapter in twenty–five meaningful words or less.

_____

_____

_____

_____

_____

_____

Dear God, I love and appreciate You because:

_____

_____

_____

Study Guide/Journal for use with Why Shofars Wail in Scripture and Today—
The Exciting Stories and Miracles!   By Mary A. Bruno, Ph.D.

152

PRAYER REQUESTS/POTENTIAL MIRACLES:

"I will answer them before they even call to me.
While they are still talking about their needs,
I will go ahead and answer their prayers!"
(Isaiah 65:24 NLT)

_____

_____

_____

_____

_____

_____

_____

_____

_____

_____

_____

_____

_____

_____

_____

_____

_____

_____

Study Guide/Journal for use with Why Shofars Wail in Scripture and Today—
The Exciting Stories and Miracles!   By Mary A. Bruno, Ph.D.

_____

_____

_____

_____

_____

_____

_____

NOTES:

_____

_____

_____

Answers: Chapter 18

1–2. (Opinion)

3. Gideon's Holy Spirit anointed shofar blasts attracted 32,000 men who were ready to fight—*for Israel*. Saul's fleshly shofar blasts drew 30,000 chariots, 6,000 men on horses, and too many men to count who were prepared to wage war—*against Israel*. Gideon's shofar instilled courage. Saul's shofar instilled fear. (p. 118)

4. It would be wise to wait for God's anointed minister to perform his/her responsibilities, and not dare to take over his/her position of authority or ministry. Saul's prideful and disrespectful actions cost him his kingdom. (pp. 119–120)

5. When Saul could no longer hear from God, he pursued ungodly counsel and went to see a medium (psychic). (pp. 120–122)

6. After Saul consulted counterfeit counsel, three of his sons died in battle; and he committed suicide—the next day—as the men of Israel fled before the Philistines and fell slain on Mount Gilboa (swollen heap). (pp. 121–122)

8–10. (Opinions)

Study Guide/Journal for use with Why Shofars Wail in Scripture and Today—
The Exciting Stories and Miracles!   By Mary A. Bruno, Ph.D.

154

Chapter 19
David and the Ark

Date: _____

The shofar was mentioned on textbook pages: 124, 125 and 126.

Events or hurdles that you have faced while focusing on this chapter:

_____

_____

_____

_____

_____

_____

_____

_____

___True: ___False:

Prior to attempting this chapter, I have asked God to give me new wisdom and understanding and to reveal all that I need to learn or change at this time.

Study Guide/Journal for use with Why Shofars Wail in Scripture and Today—
The Exciting Stories and Miracles! · By Mary A. Bruno, Ph.D.

155

POINTS TO PONDER: (Sharing your answers in class is always optional.)

1. Main characters:

_____

_____

_____

_____

2. Key words:

_____

_____

_____

_____

3. What all did King David do to usher in the Ark of the Covenant from Obed-edom's house to Jerusalem?

_____

_____

_____

_____

_____

_____

_____

_____

Study Guide/Journal for use with Why Shofars Wail in Scripture and Today—
The Exciting Stories and Miracles!   By Mary A. Bruno, Ph.D.

156

_____

_____

_____

_____

4. (Two–part question) Tell what David wore during the Ark's welcome celebration. Why do you suppose God decided to specify in His Holy Book, exactly how David was dressed?

_____

_____

_____

_____

_____

_____

_____

_____

5. What made a threefold sound of rejoicing that welcomed God during the Ark's return to Jerusalem?

_____

_____

_____

_____

_____

_____

Study Guide/Journal for use with Why Shofars Wail in Scripture and Today—
The Exciting Stories and Miracles!   By Mary A. Bruno, Ph.D.

157

_____

_____

6. How did Michael, Saul's daughter (David's wife), respond to David's efforts to praise the Lord during the Ark's return?

_____

_____

_____

_____

7. (Three-part question) What kind of family conflicts did David experience after having led a big praise celebration for God? Have you ever experienced difficult challenges during, or after, having done something special to honor God? Please explain.

_____

_____

_____

_____

_____

_____

_____

_____

_____

_____

Study Guide/Journal for use with Why Shofars Wail in Scripture and Today—
The Exciting Stories and Miracles!   By Mary A. Bruno, Ph.D.

158

_____

_____

_____

8. Lessons learned or special insights about the Lord and His loving involvement with His people.

_____

_____

_____

_____

_____

_____

_____

_____

_____

_____

_____

9. Other Scriptures, lessons, examples, or memories that came to mind while studying this chapter.

_____

_____

Study Guide/Journal for use with Why Shofars Wail in Scripture and Today—
The Exciting Stories and Miracles!   By Mary A. Bruno, Ph.D.

159

_____

_____

_____

_____

_____

_____

_____

_____

_____

10. Improve your communication skills by summarizing this chapter in twenty–five meaningful words or less.

_____

_____

_____

_____

_____

_____

Dear God, I love and appreciate You because:

_____

_____

_____

Study Guide/Journal for use with Why Shofars Wail in Scripture and Today—
The Exciting Stories and Miracles!　　　　By Mary A. Bruno, Ph.D.

160

PRAYER REQUESTS/POTENTIAL MIRACLES:

"I will answer them before they even call to me.
While they are still talking about their needs,
I will go ahead and answer their prayers!"
(Isaiah 65:24 NLT)

_____

_____

_____

_____

_____

_____

_____

_____

_____

_____

_____

_____

_____

_____

_____

_____

_____

_____

Study Guide/Journal for use with Why Shofars Wail in Scripture and Today—
The Exciting Stories and Miracles!　　　　　By Mary A. Bruno, Ph.D.

_____

_____

_____

_____

_____

_____

NOTES:

_____

_____

_____

_____

_____

_____

Answers: Chapter 19

1–2. Opinion)

3. David assembled musicians and worshipers etc., to escort the Ark to Jerusalem. (pp. 123–124)

4. David wore a robe of fine linen and an ephod of linen. God knew that a Hollywood movie would give a false representation of the event. (p. 125)

5. Shofars, trumpets, and the crowd's teruwah shout rang loud, and clear, before the Ark, and made a threefold sound of rejoicing. (p. 125)

6. Michael was disgusted with David's bold expressions of love for God. (p. 126)

7. His wife despised him, and Absalom, his son from Haggith, turned against him and tried to seize the throne. (p. 126)

8–10. (Opinion)

Study Guide/Journal for use with Why Shofars Wail in Scripture and Today—
The Exciting Stories and Miracles!   By Mary A. Bruno, Ph.D.

162

Chapter 20
Rebellious Spirits

Date: _____

The shofar was mentioned on textbook pages: 127, 129, 131, 132, 133 and 134.

Events or hurdles that you have faced while focusing on this chapter:

_____

_____

_____

_____

_____

_____

_____

_____

___True: ___False:

Prior to attempting this chapter, I have asked God to give me new wisdom and understanding and to reveal all that I need to learn or change at this time.

Study Guide/Journal for use with Why Shofars Wail in Scripture and Today—
The Exciting Stories and Miracles!   By Mary A. Bruno, Ph.D.

163

POINTS TO PONDER: (Sharing your answers in class is always optional.)

1. Main characters:

_____

_____

_____

_____

2. Key words:

_____

_____

_____

_____

3. (Two-part question) Who was fighting against whom when Joab's shofar called for peace in 2 Samuel 2:28? What happened after his shofar sounded?

_____

_____

_____

_____

_____

_____

_____

Study Guide/Journal for use with Why Shofars Wail in Scripture and Today—
The Exciting Stories and Miracles!　　　　　　　By Mary A. Bruno, Ph.D.

164

4. (Three–part question)

> "Cry aloud, spare not,
> Lift up your voice like a trumpet;
> Tell My people their transgression,
> And the house of Jacob their sins" (Isa. 58:1).

Has God ever used you to lift up your voice like a shofar to end strife and bring (or restore) peace? Explain. Do you think that "like a shofar" implies *volume*, spiritual *impact*, or something else?

_____

_____

_____

_____

_____

_____

_____

_____

_____

_____

_____

5. (Two–part question) How did King David tell Joab, Abishai, and Ittai, to deal with his defiant son, Absalom, when he tried to steal the throne? And what did Commander Joab do before blowing his shofar?

_____

_____

Study Guide/Journal for use with Why Shofars Wail in Scripture and Today—
The Exciting Stories and Miracles!   By Mary A. Bruno, Ph.D.

165

_____

_____

_____

_____

_____

_____

6. (Three-part question) What was Absalom riding when his head caught in a terebinth tree? Do you think that this scene may have hinted at what was going on in Absalom's life? Explain.

_____

_____

_____

_____

_____

_____

7. Do you suppose a spirit of rebellion may have worked in Absalom before moving on to the shofar blowing Sheba? What were the indicators that led to your answer to this question?

_____

_____

_____

_____

Study Guide/Journal for use with Why Shofars Wail in Scripture and Today—
The Exciting Stories and Miracles!   By Mary A. Bruno, Ph.D.

166

_____

_____

_____

_____

_____

8. (Two–part question) From what violations did the wise woman of Abel of Beth Maacah, and Abigail, save David and Joab? What might be a good approach to consider when having to deal with difficult people?

_____

_____

_____

_____

_____

_____

_____

9. Lessons learned or special insights about the Lord and His loving involvement with His people.

_____

_____

_____

Study Guide/Journal for use with Why Shofars Wail in Scripture and Today—
The Exciting Stories and Miracles!   By Mary A. Bruno, Ph.D.

167

_____

_____

_____

_____

_____

_____

_____

_____

_____

10. Improve your communication skills by summarizing this chapter in twenty-five meaningful words or less.

_____

_____

_____

_____

_____

Dear God, I love and appreciate You because:

_____

_____

_____

_____

Study Guide/Journal for use with Why Shofars Wail in Scripture and Today—
The Exciting Stories and Miracles!   By Mary A. Bruno, Ph.D.

168

PRAYER REQUESTS/POTENTIAL MIRACLES:

"I will answer them before they even call to me.
While they are still talking about their needs,
I will go ahead and answer their prayers!"
(Isaiah 65:24 NLT)

_____

_____

_____

_____

_____

_____

_____

_____

_____

_____

_____

_____

_____

_____

_____

_____

_____

_____

_____

Study Guide/Journal for use with Why Shofars Wail in Scripture and Today—
The Exciting Stories and Miracles!　　　　By Mary A. Bruno, Ph.D.

_____

_____

_____

_____

_____

_____

_____

NOTES:

_____

_____

_____

Answers: Chapter 20

1–2. (Opinion)

3. Brethren were fighting against brethren. They stopped trying to kill of one another. (p. 127)

4. (Opinion)

5. David told them to deal gently with his son Absalom. Joab thrust three spears into Absalom's chest, let his ten armor bearers finish him off, and then blew his own horn, which was a shofar. (pp. 127–128)

6. Absalom was riding a mule. (p. 128) (Opinion)

7. (Opinion)

8. Their wise words and actions kept David and Joab from violating their integrity. (Opinion) When dealing with a difficult person, appealing to one's sense of conscience and integrity may help. (pp. 131–132)

9–10. (Opinions)

Study Guide/Journal for use with Why Shofars Wail in Scripture and Today—
The Exciting Stories and Miracles!   By Mary A. Bruno, Ph.D.

170

Chapter 21
Solomon – Part 1

Date: _____

The shofar was mentioned on textbook page: 142.

Events or hurdles that you have faced while focusing on this chapter:

_____

_____

_____

_____

_____

_____

_____

_____

_____

___True: ___False:

Prior to attempting this chapter, I have asked God to give me new wisdom and understanding and to reveal all that I need to learn or change at this time.

Study Guide/Journal for use with Why Shofars Wail in Scripture and Today—
The Exciting Stories and Miracles!   By Mary A. Bruno, Ph.D.

171

POINTS TO PONDER: (Sharing your answers in class is always optional.)

1. Main characters:

_____

_____

_____

_____

2. Key words:

_____

_____

_____

_____

3. (Two–part question) How would you describe Adonijah's opinion of himself as he followed Absalom's example and tried to usurp David's throne? Do you think Haggith may have led her sons to believe that they would reign on David's throne?

_____

_____

_____

_____

_____

_____

Study Guide/Journal for use with Why Shofars Wail in Scripture and Today—
The Exciting Stories and Miracles!　　　　　　By Mary A. Bruno, Ph.D.

172

_____

_____

_____

4. Explain Adonijah's mindset and level of wisdom when he put Joab on his throne-stealing team. (Adonijah knew that Joab had murdered Absalom (his brother) for trying to do the same thing.) Sadly, rebellion and selfish ambition had blinded Adonijah to what could result from his foolish choices.

_____

_____

_____

_____

_____

_____

5. How did God use Nathan the prophet to protect David's throne?

_____

_____

_____

_____

_____

_____

_____

_____

Study Guide/Journal for use with Why Shofars Wail in Scripture and Today—
The Exciting Stories and Miracles! By Mary A. Bruno, Ph.D.

173

6. What was Bathsheba's attitude when she appealed to her fading king?

_____

_____

_____

_____

_____

_____

7. (Two-part question) What did David order his servants to do with Solomon in 1 Kings 34–37? What may the two horns used for Solomon's coronation, have represented?

_____

_____

_____

_____

_____

_____

_____

_____

_____

_____

Study Guide/Journal for use with Why Shofars Wail in Scripture and Today—
The Exciting Stories and Miracles!   By Mary A. Bruno, Ph.D.

174

8. (Three–part question) What happened after God's anointing flowed during Solomon's joyous coronation when wailing shofars brought breakthrough? After his coronation, who or what did Solomon confront? Tell about when you may have had to address conflict during or immediately after a big advancement, promotion, or breakthrough.

_____

_____

_____

_____

_____

_____

_____

_____

_____

_____

_____

_____

_____

_____

_____

_____

_____

_____

_____

Study Guide/Journal for use with Why Shofars Wail in Scripture and Today—
The Exciting Stories and Miracles!   By Mary A. Bruno, Ph.D.

175

9. Lessons learned or special insights about the Lord and His loving involvement with His people.

_____

_____

_____

_____

_____

_____

_____

10. Improve your communication skills by summarizing this chapter in twenty-five meaningful words or less.

_____

_____

_____

_____

_____

_____

Dear God, I love and appreciate You because:

_____

_____

_____

Study Guide/Journal for use with Why Shofars Wail in Scripture and Today—
The Exciting Stories and Miracles!   By Mary A. Bruno, Ph.D.

176

PRAYER REQUESTS/POTENTIAL MIRACLES:

"I will answer them before they even call to me.
While they are still talking about their needs,
I will go ahead and answer their prayers!"
(Isaiah 65:24 NLT)

_____

_____

_____

_____

_____

_____

_____

_____

_____

_____

_____

_____

_____

_____

_____

_____

_____

_____

*Study Guide/Journal for use with Why Shofars Wail in Scripture and Today—
The Exciting Stories and Miracles!* By Mary A. Bruno, Ph.D.

177

_____

_____

_____

_____

_____

_____

_____

NOTES:

_____

_____

_____

_____

Answers: Chapter 21

1–2. (Opinion)

3. (Opinion) (pp. 135–136)

4. (Opinion) (p. 136)

5. Nathan coached Bathsheba, the real woman behind the throne, and urged her to remind David of his promise that Solomon would be king after him. (pp. 139–142)

6. Bathsheba approached David with humility and respect while reminding him of his promise regarding Solomon. (p. 140)

7. David ordered his servants to put Solomon on the royal mule and escort him to Gihon where Zadok would anoint Solomon, king. (p. 140. The two horns may have represented a multiple anointing. (pp. 139–140)

8. Shakeups followed Solomon's anointing. He had to confront and deal with Adonijah's takeover plot. (pp. 141–142)

9–10. (Opinion)

_Study Guide/Journal for use with Why Shofars Wail in Scripture and Today—
The Exciting Stories and Miracles!_ By Mary A. Bruno, Ph.D.

178

Chapter 22
Solomon – Part 2

Date: _____

The shofar was mentioned on textbook pages: 143, 144, 151 and 152.

Events or hurdles that you have faced while focusing on this chapter:

_____

_____

_____

_____

_____

_____

_____

_____

_____

___True: ___False:

Prior to attempting this chapter, I have asked God to give me new wisdom and understanding and to reveal all that I need to learn or change at this time.

Study Guide/Journal for use with Why Shofars Wail in Scripture and Today—
The Exciting Stories and Miracles!   By Mary A. Bruno, Ph.D.

179

POINTS TO PONDER: (Sharing your answers in class is always optional.)

1. Main characters:

_____

_____

_____

_____

2. Key words:

_____

_____

_____

_____

3. Explain how shofar blasts may differently affect those who hear them.

_____

_____

_____

_____

_____

_____

_____

_____

_____

Study Guide/Journal for use with Why Shofars Wail in Scripture and Today—
The Exciting Stories and Miracles!　　　　　By Mary A. Bruno, Ph.D.

180

4. Comment on what Solomon may have felt when he had to confront his brother, who clung to the horns of the altar and begged for his life.

_____

_____

_____

_____

_____

5. What kind of relationship do you think the wise King Solomon had with Bathsheba, his mother?

_____

_____

_____

_____

6. (Three-part question) In addition to Solomon, who or what else was involved in most of King David's Seven Steps to Success? Would those steps still work today? Why?

_____

_____

_____

_____

_____

_Study Guide/Journal for use with Why Shofars Wail in Scripture and Today—
The Exciting Stories and Miracles!_   By Mary A. Bruno, Ph.D.

181

_____

_____

_____

_____

_____

_____

_____

7. Explain why David, from his deathbed, instructed Solomon to take care of the rest of David's unfinished business with Joab.

_____

_____

_____

_____

_____

_____

_____

_____

_____

8. (Two-part question) How was Bathsheba, while seated on her throne, an example of the believers in Ephesians 2:4–8? Review the tenses used in Ephesians 2:4–8. What do they reveal about a believer's place in Christ?

_____

_____

Study Guide/Journal for use with Why Shofars Wail in Scripture and Today—
The Exciting Stories and Miracles!   By Mary A. Bruno, Ph.D.

182

_____

_____

_____

_____

_____

_____

_____

_____

_____

9. Tell of other biblical passages or memories that God has brought to mind while reading this chapter, and how they relate to your life:

_____

_____

_____

_____

_____

_____

_____

_____

_____

Study Guide/Journal for use with Why Shofars Wail in Scripture and Today—
The Exciting Stories and Miracles!   By Mary A. Bruno, Ph.D.

183

_____

_____

_____

_____

_____

_____

_____

_____

10. Improve your communication skills by summarizing this chapter in twenty-five meaningful words or less.

_____

_____

_____

_____

_____

_____

Dear God, I love and appreciate You because:

_____

_____

_____

_____

_____

Study Guide/Journal for use with Why Shofars Wail in Scripture and Today—
The Exciting Stories and Miracles!   By Mary A. Bruno, Ph.D.

184

PRAYER REQUESTS/POTENTIAL MIRACLES:

"I will answer them before they even call to me.
While they are still talking about their needs,
I will go ahead and answer their prayers!"
(Isaiah 65:24 NLT)

_____
_____
_____
_____
_____
_____
_____
_____
_____
_____
_____
_____
_____
_____
_____
_____
_____
_____

*Study Guide/Journal for use with Why Shofars Wail in Scripture and Today—
The Exciting Stories and Miracles!* By Mary A. Bruno, Ph.D.

_____

_____

_____

_____

_____

_____

NOTES:

_____

_____

_____

_____

Answers: Chapter 22

1–2. (Opinion)

3. Shofar wails that brought joy to some people, terrified others. (p. 143)

4. (Opinion) (p. 148)

5. He loved and respected his mother enough to place a throne for her next to his. (Opinion) (p. 149)

6. God and His Word were involved in six of the seven steps to success that King David gave to Solomon when he was about to become King. (Opinions) (pp. 144–146)

7. David and Solomon's motives were to overthrow the power and penalty of Joab's evil crimes from David's bloodline. (p. 149)

8. Bathsheba is an example of a repentant and fully restored sinner, redeemed by God's grace. (Opinion) This passage includes past tense, present tense, and future tense. God's salvation is a gift (not earned) to all who believe. (p. 149)

9–10. (Opinion)

Study Guide/Journal for use with Why Shofars Wail in Scripture and Today—
The Exciting Stories and Miracles!   By Mary A. Bruno, Ph.D.

186

Chapter 23
Elijah and Jehu

Date: _____

The shofar was mentioned on textbook pages: 157, 158 and 160.

Events or hurdles that you have faced while focusing on this chapter:

_____

_____

_____

_____

_____

_____

_____

_____

___True: ___False:

Prior to attempting this chapter, I have asked God to give me new wisdom and understanding and to reveal all that I need to learn or change at this time.

Study Guide/Journal for use with Why Shofars Wail in Scripture and Today—
The Exciting Stories and Miracles!   By Mary A. Bruno, Ph.D.

187

POINTS TO PONDER: (Sharing your answers in class is always optional.)

1. Main characters:

_____

_____

_____

_____

2. Key words:

_____

_____

_____

_____

3. God may have enjoyed giving us a visual connection between Elijah's juniper tree (broom tree) and Jehu's upcoming *clean sweep* project. Can you share about when God may have used an example from nature, etc., to illustrate a point for you?

_____

_____

_____

_____

_____

_____

Study Guide/Journal for use with Why Shofars Wail in Scripture and Today—
The Exciting Stories and Miracles!   By Mary A. Bruno, Ph.D.

188

4. (Three–part question) How did Elijah feel regarding what God had revealed that Hazael—the man He had said to anoint king—would do to the Israelites? Did Elijah's act of anointing Hazael king, also make him responsible for Hazael's actions? Why?

_____

_____

_____

_____

_____

_____

_____

_____

5. (Two–part question) Review the mission statement that God gave Jehu. When God gives you a new position of responsibility, what else can you expect? Explain what Jehu's anointing did for him, and what it did not do.

_____

_____

_____

_____

_____

Study Guide/Journal for use with Why Shofars Wail in Scripture and Today—
The Exciting Stories and Miracles!   By Mary A. Bruno, Ph.D.

189

_____

_____

_____

_____

_____

6. (Two-part question) Were shofars involved in King Jehu's anointing? If so, who blew them and where?

_____

_____

_____

_____

_____

_____

_____

_____

7. What kind of (or size) container would have been adequate for disposing of Jezebel's remains?

_____

_____

_____

_____

_____

Study Guide/Journal for use with Why Shofars Wail in Scripture and Today—
The Exciting Stories and Miracles!   By Mary A. Bruno, Ph.D.

190

8. (Three–part question) How did God reward Jehu's job performance? When your ways please the Lord, what kind of blessing do you think God will pour out on your family and on future generations of your bloodline? Dare to expect God's best for them. What did the diligent dogs get out of the Jezebel episode?

_____

_____

_____

_____

_____

_____

_____

_____

_____

_____

_____

9. Lessons learned, and insights or comments regarding this chapter.

_____

_____

_____

_____

_____

Study Guide/Journal for use with Why Shofars Wail in Scripture and Today—
The Exciting Stories and Miracles!   By Mary A. Bruno, Ph.D.

191

_____

_____

_____

_____

_____

_____

_____

_____

_____

10. Improve your communication skills by summarizing this chapter in twenty–five meaningful words or less.

_____

_____

_____

_____

_____

_____

Dear God, I love and appreciate You because:

_____

_____

_____

Study Guide/Journal for use with Why Shofars Wail in Scripture and Today—
The Exciting Stories and Miracles!   By Mary A. Bruno, Ph.D.

192

PRAYER REQUESTS/POTENTIAL MIRACLES:

"I will answer them before they even call to me.
While they are still talking about their needs,
I will go ahead and answer their prayers!"
(Isaiah 65:24 NLT)

_____
_____
_____
_____
_____
_____
_____
_____
_____
_____
_____
_____
_____
_____
_____
_____
_____
_____

Study Guide/Journal for use with Why Shofars Wail in Scripture and Today—
The Exciting Stories and Miracles!   By Mary A. Bruno, Ph.D.

193

_____

_____

_____

_____

_____

_____

NOTES:

_____

_____

_____

_____

Answers: Chapter 23

1–2. (Opinion)

3. (Opinion)

4. Elisha wept. (Opinion) He was only responsible for obeying God's anointing orders, because, God had told Elijah to anoint Hazael king. (p. 154) Elisha had acted on God's orders.

5. We can expect God's direction and power to equip us to fill a position and complete an assignment. Jehu's anointing set him apart and equipped him, but it did not make him righteous. (p. 156)

6. Yes, a shofar sounded when Jehu was anointed king. His officers blew the shofar, by the (anointed) steps and announced: "Jehu is king!" (p. 157)

7. (Opinion) A wastebasket, perhaps. (p. 159)

8. God commended Jehu for doing what was right in His sight and promised that Jehu's children of the fourth generation would sit on Israel's throne. The dogs got a spicy meal and honorable mention in God's Book. (p. 160)

9–10. (Opinion)

Study Guide/Journal for use with Why Shofars Wail in Scripture and Today—
The Exciting Stories and Miracles!   By Mary A. Bruno, Ph.D.

194

Chapter 24
Crumbled Walls

Date: _____

The shofar was mentioned on textbook pages: 161, 165, 166, 167 and 168.

Events or hurdles that you have faced while focusing on this chapter:

_____

_____

_____

_____

_____

_____

_____

_____

___True: ___False:

Prior to attempting this chapter, I have asked God to give me new wisdom and understanding and to reveal all that I need to learn or change at this time.

Study Guide/Journal for use with Why Shofars Wail in Scripture and Today—
The Exciting Stories and Miracles!   By Mary A. Bruno, Ph.D.

195

POINTS TO PONDER: (Sharing your answers in class is always optional.)

1. Main characters:

_____

_____

_____

_____

2. Key words:

_____

_____

_____

_____

3. Nehemiah was an extraordinary man who interacted daily with royalty. What kind of room did he make for prayer, if any, in his busy schedule?

_____

_____

_____

_____

_____

_____

_____

Study Guide/Journal for use with Why Shofars Wail in Scripture and Today—
The Exciting Stories and Miracles!   By Mary A. Bruno, Ph.D.

196

4. Nehemiah had to be at his best when serving the king. Do you think he dared to risk fasting while presenting his petitions before God? Why?

_____

_____

_____

_____

_____

5. (Two–part question) How much time passed between Nehemiah's intense prayer, and when the king gave him the time off, permits, and provisions? What does this tell you about God's answers to your prayers?

_____

_____

_____

_____

_____

_____

_____

_____

_____

_____

_____

Study Guide/Journal for use with Why Shofars Wail in Scripture and Today—
The Exciting Stories and Miracles!   By Mary A. Bruno, Ph.D.

197

6. (Two–part question) In addition to enough materials to rebuild Jerusalem's walls, what did Nehemiah get to build for his personal needs? Please write Philippians 4:19.

_____

_____

_____

_____

_____

_____

_____

7. (Two–part question) When did Nehemiah's promotion to governor occur? What does this reveal about God's timing for blessings that come after fasting and prayer?

_____

_____

_____

_____

_____

_____

_____

Study Guide/Journal for use with Why Shofars Wail in Scripture and Today—
The Exciting Stories and Miracles!   By Mary A. Bruno, Ph.D.

198

8. (Three–part question) Please write Nehemiah 4:20 in the space provided below. Do you think shofar blasts still send that message of hope for believers today? Please explain.

_____

_____

_____

_____

_____

_____

_____

_____

_____

9. Lessons learned or special insights about the Lord and His loving involvement with His people.

_____

_____

_____

_____

_____

_____

_____

Study Guide/Journal for use with Why Shofars Wail in Scripture and Today—
The Exciting Stories and Miracles! By Mary A. Bruno, Ph.D.

199

_____

_____

_____

_____

_____

_____

_____

_____

10. Challenge yourself and polish your communication skills by summarizing this chapter in twenty-five meaningful words or less.

_____

_____

_____

_____

_____

_____

_____

Dear God, I love and appreciate You because:

_____

_____

_____

_____

Study Guide/Journal for use with Why Shofars Wail in Scripture and Today—
The Exciting Stories and Miracles!   By Mary A. Bruno, Ph.D.

200

PRAYER REQUESTS/POTENTIAL MIRACLES:

"I will answer them before they even call to me.
While they are still talking about their needs,
I will go ahead and answer their prayers!"
(Isaiah 65:24 NLT)

_____

_____

_____

_____

_____

_____

_____

_____

_____

_____

_____

_____

_____

_____

_____

_____

_____

_____

_____

Study Guide/Journal for use with Why Shofars Wail in Scripture and Today—
The Exciting Stories and Miracles!   By Mary A. Bruno, Ph.D.

201

_____

_____

_____

_____

_____

NOTES:

_____

_____

_____

_____

Answers: Chapter 24

1–2. (Opinion)

3. Nehemiah poured out his heart to God in prayer (with tears) as he cited God's promises. (pp. 161–162)

4. (Opinion) Nehemiah included fasting with his prayer. (p. 162)

5. About 4–5 months had passed between Nehemiah's initial prayer request and when God's answer came. (November/December to March/April) (pp. 162) (Opinion)

6. Nehemiah got to build a house for himself. (p. 164), "And my God shall supply all your need according to His riches in glory by Christ Jesus" (Philippians 4:19).

7. Nehemiah's promotion to governor came in the same year as his fasting and prayer. (p. 164) God's answers and blessings may not arrive immediately after our prayer—but they will be on the way.

8. (Opinion) Shofar blasts remind us that God still fights for His own. (pp. 167–168)

"Wherever you hear the sound of the trumpet, rally to us there. Our God will fight for us" (Nehemiah 4:20).

9–10. (Opinion)

Study Guide/Journal for use with Why Shofars Wail in Scripture and Today—
The Exciting Stories and Miracles!   By Mary A. Bruno, Ph.D.

202

Chapter 25

Five Insights

Date: _____

The shofar was mentioned on textbook pages: 169, 170, 171, 172, 173, 174, 175, 176, 177, and 178.

Events or hurdles that you have faced while focusing on this chapter:

_____

_____

_____

_____

_____

_____

_____

_____

___True: ___False:

Prior to attempting this chapter, I have asked God to give me new wisdom and understanding and to reveal all that I need to learn or change at this time.

Study Guide/Journal for use with Why Shofars Wail in Scripture and Today—
The Exciting Stories and Miracles!   By Mary A. Bruno, Ph.D.

203

POINTS TO PONDER: (Sharing your answers in class is always optional.)

1. Main characters:

_____

_____

_____

_____

2. Key words:

_____

_____

_____

_____

3. Explain the translated forms of the word *clap (taqua), and* why the Scriptures urge believers to clap their hands and praise God.

_____

_____

_____

_____

_____

_____

_____

Study Guide/Journal for use with Why Shofars Wail in Scripture and Today—
The Exciting Stories and Miracles!　　　　　　　By Mary A. Bruno, Ph.D.

204

_____

_____

_____

4. Based on these translations of the word *clap*, which include *blowing a trumpet or shofar,* what kind of impact does our chapping and praise convey?

_____

_____

_____

_____

_____

_____

_____

_____

_____

5. With what kind of shout did God go up in Psalms 47:5?

_____

_____

_____

_____

_____

Study Guide/Journal for use with Why Shofars Wail in Scripture and Today—
The Exciting Stories and Miracles!   By Mary A. Bruno, Ph.D.

205

6. (Three-part question) What are the meanings of the words, *sing, shout,* and *trumpet* in Psalm 81:1–4?

_____

_____

_____

_____

_____

_____

_____

_____

_____

_____

_____

_____

_____

_____

_____

_____

_____

7. Comment on whose idea it was (and why) for believers to blow shofars and shout joyfully before the Lord, in Psalms 81:1–4, 98:6, and 150:3–5.

_____

_____

_____

Study Guide/Journal for use with Why Shofars Wail in Scripture and Today—
The Exciting Stories and Miracles!   By Mary A. Bruno, Ph.D.

206

_____

_____

_____

8. (Two–part question) Would dancing and singing accompanied by shaking tambourines, blaring shofars, and high-sounding cymbals, be welcomed at your place of worship? Why?

_____

_____

_____

_____

_____

_____

_____

9. Lessons learned, and what needs to change in my life:

_____

_____

_____

_____

_____

_____

_____

Study Guide/Journal for use with Why Shofars Wail in Scripture and Today—
The Exciting Stories and Miracles!   By Mary A. Bruno, Ph.D.

207

_____

_____

_____

_____

_____

_____

_____

10. Improve your communication skills by summarizing this chapter in twenty–five meaningful words or less.

_____

_____

_____

_____

_____

Dear God, I love and appreciate You because:

_____

_____

_____

_____

_____

Study Guide/Journal for use with Why Shofars Wail in Scripture and Today—
The Exciting Stories and Miracles!   By Mary A. Bruno, Ph.D.

208

PRAYER REQUESTS/POTENTIAL MIRACLES:

I will answer them before they even call to me.
While they are still talking about their needs,
I will go ahead and answer their prayers!"
(Isaiah 65:24 NLT)

_____

_____

_____

_____

_____

_____

_____

_____

_____

_____

_____

_____

_____

_____

_____

_____

*Study Guide/Journal for use with Why Shofars Wail in Scripture and Today—
The Exciting Stories and Miracles!*   By Mary A. Bruno, Ph.D.

209

_____

_____

_____

_____

_____

_____

_____

_____

NOTES:

_____

_____

_____

Answers: Chapter 25

1–2. (Opinion)

3. Clapping, a form of praise, is also a form of spiritual warfare. (p. 171)

4. Our clapping has the same kind of impact as worship, blowing a shofar, or thrusting a weapon. (p. 172)

5. God went up with a Teruwah shout—the alarm, battle cry, a shout of joy, and Jubilee shout—a shofar blast. (p. 172)

6. Sing for joy, *ranan,* means, "To overcome, cry out, shout for joy, and give a ringing cry." Shout joyfully, *ruwa,* means "shout, noise, alarm, cry, triumph, and to shout, raise a sound, cry out, give a blast, to shout a war cry or alarm of battle, shout in triumph, and shout in applause." The trumpet was a *shofar.* (pp. 173–174)

7. (Opinion) It was God's idea for His people to blow shofars and shout joyfully before Him. (pp. 176–178)

8–10. (Opinion)

Study Guide/Journal for use with Why Shofars Wail in Scripture and Today—
The Exciting Stories and Miracles!   By Mary A. Bruno, Ph.D.

210

Chapter 26
Isaiah and Jeremiah

Date: _____

The shofar was mentioned on textbook pages: 179, 180, 182, 183, and 184.

Events or hurdles that you have faced while focusing on this chapter:

_____
_____
_____
_____
_____
_____
_____
_____
_____

___True: ___False:

Prior to attempting this chapter, I have asked God to give me new wisdom and understanding and to reveal all that I need to learn or change at this time.

Study Guide/Journal for use with Why Shofars Wail in Scripture and Today— The Exciting Stories and Miracles!
By Mary A. Bruno, Ph.D.

211

POINTS TO PONDER: (Sharing your answers in class is always optional.)

1. Main characters:

_____

_____

_____

_____

2. Key words:

_____

_____

_____

_____

3. (Two–part question) According to Isaiah 18:3b, what are we to do when the shofar is blown? Why is this important?

_____

_____

_____

_____

_____

_____

_____

_____

Study Guide/Journal for use with Why Shofars Wail in Scripture and Today—
The Exciting Stories and Miracles!   By Mary A. Bruno, Ph.D.

212

4. (Two-part question) Why does God urge to "lift up your voice like a trumpet (shofar)" in Isaiah 58:1? Are you ready to do so?

_____

_____

_____

_____

_____

_____

_____

5. (Two-part question) How does God feel about those who have wandered far away from Him and have ended up on bondage? Please give Scripture(s) to support your answer.

_____

_____

_____

_____

_____

_____

_____

_____

_____

Study Guide/Journal for use with Why Shofars Wail in Scripture and Today—
The Exciting Stories and Miracles!   By Mary A. Bruno, Ph.D.

213

6. (Three–part question) In Jeremiah 6:17, who urged God's people to listen to the sound of the trumpet (shofar)? Have you ever heard anyone urge a congregation to pay attention to the sound of a shofar? Is so, when, where, and why? How often do shofars sound in your house of worship?

_____

_____

_____

_____

_____

_____

_____

_____

_____

_____

7. What does Jeremiah 51:27 urge to do to lift up a signal to the nations?

_____

_____

_____

_____

Study Guide/Journal for use with Why Shofars Wail in Scripture and Today—
The Exciting Stories and Miracles!   By Mary A. Bruno, Ph.D.

214

8. (Two–part question) Of whom do you think the Lord speaks when He uses the word "Us" in Isaiah 6:8? Tell about when you may have heard God's call to go for Him, and answered, "Here am I. Send me."

_____

_____

_____

_____

_____

_____

_____

_____

_____

_____

_____

_____

9. Lessons learned or special insights about the Lord and His loving involvement with His people.

_____

_____

Study Guide/Journal for use with Why Shofars Wail in Scripture and Today—
The Exciting Stories and Miracles!   By Mary A. Bruno, Ph.D.

215

_____

_____

_____

_____

_____

_____

_____

_____

_____

_____

10. Improve your communication skills by summarizing this chapter in twenty-five meaningful words or less.

_____

_____

_____

_____

_____

_____

Dear God, I love and appreciate You because:

_____

_____

_____

Study Guide/Journal for use with Why Shofars Wail in Scripture and Today—
The Exciting Stories and Miracles!   By Mary A. Bruno, Ph.D.

216

PRAYER REQUESTS/POTENTIAL MIRACLES:

"I will answer them before they even call to me.
While they are still talking about their needs,
I will go ahead and answer their prayers!"
(Isaiah 65:24 NLT)

_____

_____

_____

_____

_____

_____

_____

_____

_____

_____

_____

_____

_____

_____

_____

_____

_____

_____

_____

_____

Study Guide/Journal for use with Why Shofars Wail in Scripture and Today—
The Exciting Stories and Miracles!   By Mary A. Bruno, Ph.D.

217

_____

_____

_____

_____

_____

_____

NOTES:

_____

_____

_____

_____

_____

Answers: Chapter 26

1–2. (Opinion)

3. We are supposed to listen when the shofar sounds. (Opinion) Shofars send messages from God that will help us. (p. 179)

4. God wants our voices to have shofar impact that will help the wandering ones to find the way back to Him. (p. 180)

5. God loves those who are in bondage and has commissioned us to set them free. Isaiah 58:1, John 3:16–17, etc. (p. 181)

6. God sent watchmen to urge people to listen to the sound of the trumpet. (p. 183) (Opinion)

7. Jeremiah urges to blow a trumpet (shofar) as a warning (signal). (p. 183)

8. (Opinion) The Holy Trinity is implied in Isaiah 6:8. (Opinion) (p. 184)

9–10. (Opinion)

Study Guide/Journal for use with Why Shofars Wail in Scripture and Today—
The Exciting Stories and Miracles!   By Mary A. Bruno, Ph.D.

218

Chapter 27
Warning!

Date: _____

The shofar was mentioned on textbook pages: 185, 186, 187, 188, and 189.

Events or hurdles that you have faced while focusing on this chapter:

_____

_____

_____

_____

_____

_____

_____

_____

___True: ___False:

Prior to attempting this chapter, I have asked God to give me new wisdom and understanding and to reveal all that I need to learn or change at this time.

Study Guide/Journal for use with Why Shofars Wail in Scripture and Today—
The Exciting Stories and Miracles!   By Mary A. Bruno, Ph.D.

219

POINTS TO PONDER: (Sharing your answers in class is always optional.)

1. Main characters:

_____

_____

_____

_____

2. Key words:

_____

_____

_____

_____

3. (Four–part question) What are the watchman's responsibilities mentioned in Ezekiel 33:1–6, and why must he sound warnings? Has God ever urged you to give anyone a spiritual warning or to speak a strong passage of Scripture to someone? Did you follow through? Explain.

_____

_____

_____

_____

_____

_____

Study Guide/Journal for use with Why Shofars Wail in Scripture and Today—
The Exciting Stories and Miracles!   By Mary A. Bruno, Ph.D.

220

_____

_____

_____

_____

_____

_____

_____

_____

_____

_____

_____

_____

_____

_____

4. What made the people vulnerable to enemy attack in Hosea 8:1?

_____

_____

_____

_____

_____

_____

Study Guide/Journal for use with Why Shofars Wail in Scripture and Today—
The Exciting Stories and Miracles!   By Mary A. Bruno, Ph.D.

221

5. (Two-part question) Have you ever let the things of God slide in your life, and then noticed that problems arose? Explain.

_____

_____

_____

_____

_____

_____

_____

_____

_____

6. (Four-part question) Why does Joel 2:1 say to, "Blow the trumpet (shofar) in Zion,"? According to Joel 2:15–16, how is blowing a shofar involved with fasting? Do you think that God wants or expects you to fast and pray for your nation to repent before Him? If you have never fasted and prayed for your nation, are you willing to do so as God's Spirit leads?

_____

_____

_____

_____

_____

_____

_____

Study Guide/Journal for use with Why Shofars Wail in Scripture and Today—
The Exciting Stories and Miracles!   By Mary A. Bruno, Ph.D.

222

_____

_____

_____

_____

7. (Two–part question) Have you heard any shofars wailing recently before or during a fast; if so, when and where?

_____

_____

_____

_____

_____

_____

_____

_____

_____

_____

8. Who is the shofar blower and defender of Zechariah 9:14–15a?

_____

_____

_____

_____

_____

_____

Study Guide/Journal for use with Why Shofars Wail in Scripture and Today—
The Exciting Stories and Miracles! By Mary A. Bruno, Ph.D.

223

9. Discuss other biblical passages, examples, or memories that came to mind while studying this chapter, and what action(s) God may want you to take regarding them.

_____

_____

_____

_____

_____

_____

10. Improve your communication skills by summarizing this chapter in twenty–five meaningful words or less.

_____

_____

_____

_____

_____

Dear God, I love and appreciate You because:

_____

_____

_____

Study Guide/Journal for use with Why Shofars Wail in Scripture and Today—
The Exciting Stories and Miracles!   By Mary A. Bruno, Ph.D.

224

PRAYER REQUESTS/POTENTIAL MIRACLES:

"I will answer them before they even call to me.
While they are still talking about their needs,
I will go ahead and answer their prayers!"
(Isaiah 65:24 NLT)

_____

_____

_____

_____

_____

_____

_____

_____

_____

_____

_____

_____

_____

_____

_____

_____

Study Guide/Journal for use with Why Shofars Wail in Scripture and Today—
The Exciting Stories and Miracles!   By Mary A. Bruno, Ph.D.

225

_____

_____

_____

_____

_____

_____

_____

_____

_____

NOTES:

_____

_____

_____

Answers: Chapter 27

1–2. (Opinion)

3. The watchman would be accountable for the people's blood if he did not warn them. (Opinions) (p. 185)

4. Sin against God made the people vulnerable to enemy attack. (Opinion) (p. 186)

5. (Opinion)

6. The shofar sounded to announce the day of the Lord is coming. (Opinion) It is scriptural to launch a fast with shofar blasts. (pp. 186–187)

7. (Opinion)

8. The Lord Himself will blow the trumpet (shofar) and defend His people. (p. 189)

9–10. (Opinion)

Study Guide/Journal for use with Why Shofars Wail in Scripture and Today—
The Exciting Stories and Miracles!   By Mary A. Bruno, Ph.D.

226

Chapter 28
Shofar Blasts Predicted – Part 1

Date: _____

The shofar was mentioned on textbook pages: 191, 192, 193, 194, 195, 196, 197 and 198.

Events or hurdles that you have faced while focusing on this chapter:

_____

_____

_____

_____

_____

_____

_____

_____

___True: ___False:

Prior to attempting this chapter, I have asked God to give me new wisdom and understanding and to reveal all that I need to learn or change at this time.

Study Guide/Journal for use with Why Shofars Wail in Scripture and Today—
The Exciting Stories and Miracles!　　　　By Mary A. Bruno, Ph.D.

227

POINTS TO PONDER: (Sharing your answers in class is always optional.)

1. Main characters:

_____

_____

_____

_____

2. Key words:

_____

_____

_____

_____

3. Comment on what Pastor Shawn Brix wrote regarding what was happening with lambs and shofars in the hour that Jesus Christ (Yeshua)—the Messiah—the Lamb of God died on the cross.

_____

_____

_____

_____

_____

_____

_____

Study Guide/Journal for use with Why Shofars Wail in Scripture and Today—
The Exciting Stories and Miracles!   By Mary A. Bruno, Ph.D.

228

_____

_____

_____

_____

_____

_____

_____

_____

_____

4. (Two–part question) What is The Great Trumpet in Matthew 24:31, and why does it sound?

_____

_____

_____

_____

_____

_____

_____

5. Whose shofar is mentioned in 1 Thessalonians 4:16–17?

_____

_____

Study Guide/Journal for use with Why Shofars Wail in Scripture and Today—
The Exciting Stories and Miracles!   By Mary A. Bruno, Ph.D.

229

_____

_____

6. (Two–part question) Explain the meaning of the *rousing cry.* Which events are mentioned in that passage?

_____

_____

_____

_____

_____

_____

_____

_____

_____

_____

_____

_____

7. (Three–part question) What did Jesus' words sound like to John when he was on the Isle of Patmos? According to Revelation 8:3–5, where are the prayers of all the saints? "All" means "all," which includes your prayers. Could it be that the voice of all of our agreeing prayers still calls, as shofars in symphony, for God's mercy and intervention from that holy altar? With that in mind, consider and comment on the following verse:

Study Guide/Journal for use with Why Shofars Wail in Scripture and Today—
The Exciting Stories and Miracles! By Mary A. Bruno, Ph.D.

230

"The effective, fervent prayer of a righteous man avails much"
(James 5:16b)

_____

_____

_____

_____

_____

_____

_____

_____

8. What will happen when an angel hurls fire from God's altar upon the earth?

_____

_____

_____

_____

_____

_____

_____

_____

Study Guide/Journal for use with Why Shofars Wail in Scripture and Today—
The Exciting Stories and Miracles!   By Mary A. Bruno, Ph.D.

231

9. Discuss other biblical passages or memories that came to mind while studying this chapter, and what action(s) God may want you to take.

_____

_____

_____

_____

_____

_____

_____

_____

10. Improve your communication skills by summarizing this chapter in twenty-five meaningful words or less.

_____

_____

_____

_____

_____

_____

Dear God, I love and appreciate You because:

_____

_____

_____

Study Guide/Journal for use with Why Shofars Wail in Scripture and Today—
The Exciting Stories and Miracles!   By Mary A. Bruno, Ph.D.

232

PRAYER REQUESTS/POTENTIAL MIRACLES:

"I will answer them before they even call to me.
While they are still talking about their needs,
I will go ahead and answer their prayers!"
(Isaiah 65:24 NLT)

_____

_____

_____

_____

_____

_____

_____

_____

_____

_____

_____

_____

_____

_____

_____

_____

_____

_____

*Study Guide/Journal for use with Why Shofars Wail in Scripture and Today—
The Exciting Stories and Miracles!*   By Mary A. Bruno, Ph.D.

233

_____

_____

_____

_____

_____

_____

NOTES:

_____

_____

_____

Answers: Chapter 28

1–2. (Opinion

3. (Opinion) Shofars sounded as Jesus (Yeshua)—God's Lamb—and the other lambs drew their last breaths. (pp. 191–192)

4. That Great Trumpet in Matthew 24:31 is a shofar. It will sound to call God's elect from all the earth. (p. 192)

5. First Thessalonians 4:16–17 speaks of God's shofar. (p. 193)

6. The _rousing cry_ can mean a command, order, stimulating cry, a summons, or trumpet call. This passage mentions the resurrection of those who have died in Christ; and the catching up of believers who are still alive at the Lord's return. (pp. 193–194)

7. Jesus' words sounded to John like the blast of a shofar. (pp. 195–196). The prayers of all the saints—all of them—are on God's golden altar, which is before His throne. (p. 197–198) (Opinion)

8. When an angel throws fire from God's altar to Earth, peals of thunder, sounds, flashes of lightning, and an earthquake will follow. (p. 198)

9–10. (Opinion)

Study Guide/Journal for use with Why Shofars Wail in Scripture and Today—
The Exciting Stories and Miracles!   By Mary A. Bruno, Ph.D.

234

Chapter 29
Shofar Blasts Predicted – Part 2

Date: _____

The shofar was mentioned on textbook pages: 199, 200, 201, 202, 203, 204, 205, and 206.

Events or hurdles that you have faced while focusing on this chapter:

_____

_____

_____

_____

_____

_____

_____

___True: ___False:

Prior to attempting this chapter, I have asked God to give me new wisdom and understanding and to reveal all that I need to learn or change at this time.

Study Guide/Journal for use with Why Shofars Wail in Scripture and Today—
The Exciting Stories and Miracles!   By Mary A. Bruno, Ph.D.

235

POINTS TO PONDER: (Sharing your answers in class is always optional.)

1. Main characters:

_____

_____

_____

_____

2. Key words:

_____

_____

_____

_____

3. (Two–part question) What will people on earth experience after the first angel (Revelation 8:7) sounds his shofar? What might you and your community do to protect yourselves if that event happened where you live?

_____

_____

_____

_____

_____

_____

_____

Study Guide/Journal for use with Why Shofars Wail in Scripture and Today—
The Exciting Stories and Miracles! By Mary A. Bruno, Ph.D.

236

4. (Two–part question) What will happen on earth when the second angel sounds his shofar in Revelation 8:8–9? How do you think the results will affect life and businesses on earth?

_____

_____

_____

_____

_____

_____

_____

5. (Two–part question) What will happen after the third angel sounds his shofar? How do you think people may try to survive?

_____

_____

_____

_____

_____

_____

_____

_____

Study Guide/Journal for use with Why Shofars Wail in Scripture and Today—
The Exciting Stories and Miracles!   By Mary A. Bruno, Ph.D.

237

6. Things get more serious with each angel's shofar blast. Discuss what people may do to stay safe after the fourth angel blows his shofar.

_____

_____

_____

_____

_____

_____

_____

_____

7. (Two–part question) Explain what will happen and how people may try to protect themselves and their children after the fifth angel's shofar wails. How long will that misery last?

_____

_____

_____

_____

_____

_____

_____

_____

Study Guide/Journal for use with Why Shofars Wail in Scripture and Today—
The Exciting Stories and Miracles!   By Mary A. Bruno, Ph.D.

238

_____

_____

_____

_____

8. (Two–part question) What will the sixth angel's shofar blast release on earth? How do you think people may try to protect themselves and their families?

_____

_____

_____

_____

_____

_____

_____

_____

9. (Two–part question) What will the seventh angel's shofar blast announce? What will life be like for those living on earth?

_____

_____

_____

_____

Study Guide/Journal for use with Why Shofars Wail in Scripture and Today—
The Exciting Stories and Miracles!   By Mary A. Bruno, Ph.D.

239

_____

_____

_____

_____

_____

_____

_____

_____

_____

_____

10. Improve your communication skills by summarizing this chapter in twenty–five meaningful words or less.

_____

_____

_____

_____

_____

_____

Dear God, I love and appreciate You because:

_____

_____

_____

Study Guide/Journal for use with Why Shofars Wail in Scripture and Today—
The Exciting Stories and Miracles!   By Mary A. Bruno, Ph.D.

240

PRAYER REQUESTS/POTENTIAL MIRACLES:

"I will answer them before they even call to me.
While they are still talking about their needs,
I will go ahead and answer their prayers!"
(Isaiah 65:24 NLT)

_____

_____

_____

_____

_____

_____

_____

_____

_____

_____

_____

_____

_____

_____

_____

_____

_____

_____

_____

_____

Study Guide/Journal for use with Why Shofars Wail in Scripture and Today—
The Exciting Stories and Miracles! By Mary A. Bruno, Ph.D.

Answers: Chapter 29

1–2. (Opinion)

3. Hail, fire, and blood will make a smelly mess and destroy a third of earth's vegetation. (Opinion) (p. 199)

4. What looks like an enormous blazing mountain will be hurled into the sea; a third of the sea will be turned into blood; a third of the sea creatures will die; and a third of the ships will be ruined. (Opinion) (p. 200)

5. A great star named "Bitterness," that blazes like a torch will fall from the sky and turn the rivers and springs bitter. People will die from drinking the bitter water. (Opinion on how to survive) (p. 200)

6. A third of the sun, moon, and stars, will grow dim. "Day and night will be a third darker. Crime will increase. (Opinion) (p. 201)

7. Billows of smoke from the abyss will darken the sun and sky with locusts that have power like scorpions, and will cause serious respiratory problems for many. The locusts will inflict pain for five months. (Opinion) (p. 202)

8. A _Two hundred million_ man death squad will kill billions of people. (Survival suggestions) (p. 203)

9. This shofar blast will announce, "The kingdom of our Lord and his Messiah, and he will rule forever and ever." Those with God's seal will rejoice.

> But the rest of mankind, who were not killed by these plagues, did not repent of the works of their hands, that they should not worship demons, and idols of gold, silver, brass, stone, and wood, which can neither see nor hear nor walk. And they did not repent of their murders or their sorceries or their sexual immorality or their thefts.
>
> —Rev. 9:20–21

Those without God's seal must endure what follows in the book of Revelation. (p. 204)

10. (Opinion)

Study Guide/Journal for use with Why Shofars Wail in Scripture and Today—
The Exciting Stories and Miracles!   By Mary A. Bruno, Ph.D.

Chapter 30

How to Lift up Your Voice as a Shofar

(How to Lead a Soul to Peace With God)

Date: _____

The shofar was mentioned on textbook pages: 207, 209 and 218.

Events or hurdles that you have faced while focusing on this chapter:

_____

_____

_____

_____

_____

_____

_____

_____

___True: ___False:

Prior to attempting this chapter, I have asked God to give me new wisdom and understanding and to reveal all that I need to learn or change at this time.

Study Guide/Journal for use with Why Shofars Wail in Scripture and Today—
The Exciting Stories and Miracles!   By Mary A. Bruno, Ph.D.

243

POINTS TO PONDER: (Sharing your answers in class is always optional.)

1. Main characters:

_____

_____

_____

_____

2. Key words:

_____

_____

_____

_____

3. (Two–part question) Explain the serious problem that stems from sin. Why do we need to get rid of it?

_____

_____

_____

_____

_____

_____

_____

Study Guide/Journal for use with Why Shofars Wail in Scripture and Today—
The Exciting Stories and Miracles!   By Mary A. Bruno, Ph.D.

244

4. (Three–part question) What became of some of the fornicators, idolaters, adulterers, effeminate, homosexuals, thieves, covetous [jealous/greedy/envious], drunkards, revilers, and swindlers, in 1 Corinthians 6:9b–11? Did they get what they deserved? Do you think this was fair?

_____

_____

_____

_____

_____

_____

_____

_____

_____

_____

_____

_____

_____

5. (Three–part question) How many sins does it take to be a sinner? What does John 3:3 say must happen before we can enter God's kingdom? Has that happened yet for you?

_____

_____

_____

_____

Study Guide/Journal for use with Why Shofars Wail in Scripture and Today—
The Exciting Stories and Miracles! By Mary A. Bruno, Ph.D.

245

_____

_____

_____

_____

_____

_____

_____

6. (Two–part question) If you agree with, John 3:16–17, and Romans 10:9, what does Roman 10:9 say will happen to you? Do you believe that to be true?

_____

_____

_____

_____

_____

_____

_____

_____

_____

_____

_____

_____

_____

_____

Study Guide/Journal for use with Why Shofars Wail in Scripture and Today—
The Exciting Stories and Miracles!   By Mary A. Bruno, Ph.D.

246

7. (Three–part question) What does Jesus say that He will do for you after you have conferred Him? What will he do for those who do not confess Him? Comment on if you have ever prayed a prayer similar to the one on page 243 244 of the textbook, or have you helped anyone to pray to receive Christ

_____

_____

_____

_____

_____

_____

_____

8. Have you told Jesus Christ, (Yeshua)—the Messiah—the Lamb of God—that you are receiving Him as your Lord and Savior? If you have not received Him yet, you are cordially invited to pause and do so right now. Please document your decision, (write the date and time) on the lines below. And then, be sure to write in the front of your Bible, the date and time that you told the Lord Jesus Christ that you were receiving Him as your Savior. This will be the most important decision of your entire life.

_____

_____

_____

_____

_____

_____

Study Guide/Journal for use with Why Shofars Wail in Scripture and Today—
The Exciting Stories and Miracles!   By Mary A. Bruno, Ph.D.

247

9. Lessons learned, and insights or comments regarding this chapter.

_____

_____

_____

_____

_____

_____

_____

_____

10. Improve your communication skills by summarizing this chapter in twenty–five meaningful words or less.

_____

_____

_____

_____

_____

_____

Dear God, I love and appreciate You because:

_____

_____

_____

Study Guide/Journal for use with Why Shofars Wail in Scripture and Today—
The Exciting Stories and Miracles!   By Mary A. Bruno, Ph.D.

248

PRAYER REQUESTS/POTENTIAL MIRACLES:

"I will answer them before they even call to me.
While they are still talking about their needs,
I will go ahead and answer their prayers!"
(Isaiah 65:24 NLT)

_____
_____
_____
_____
_____
_____
_____
_____
_____
_____
_____
_____
_____
_____
_____
_____
_____
_____

Study Guide/Journal for use with Why Shofars Wail in Scripture and Today—
The Exciting Stories and Miracles! By Mary A. Bruno, Ph.D.

249

_____

_____

_____

_____

_____

_____

NOTES:

_____

_____

_____

_____

Answers: Chapter 30

1–2. (Opinion)

3. Retained sin will keep us out of heaven. (pp. 207–208)

4. They were justified [just as if they had never sinned] in the name of the Lord Jesus Christ and in the Spirit of God. (p. 208) (Opinion)

5. Ordinarily, it would only take one sin to make one sinner. However, we were born with sin from Adam and Eve already at work in our bloodline. This is why Jesus said, "Unless one is born again, he cannot see the kingdom of God." (John 3:3) (pp. 208–209)

6. (Opinion) Those who believe and receive Christ will be saved. (Opinion) (pp. 209–210)

7. Jesus will confess (claim) you before His Father, who is in heaven—if you confess (claim) Him. However, if you deny Him, He will also deny you. (p. 212) (Opinion)

8. (Opinions) (Tell Jesus that you are receiving Him at this very moment.) (p. 215–216)

9–10. (Opinion)

Study Guide/Journal for use with Why Shofars Wail in Scripture and Today—
The Exciting Stories and Miracles! By Mary A. Bruno, Ph.D.

250

Chapter 31
Shofar Trip – Part 1: Northern Route

Date: _____

The shofar was mentioned on textbook pages: 219, 220, 221, 222, 223, 224, and 226.

Events or hurdles that you have faced while focusing on this chapter:

_____

_____

_____

_____

_____

_____

_____

_____

___True: ___False:

Prior to attempting this chapter, I have asked God to give me new wisdom and understanding and to reveal all that I need to learn or change at this time.

Study Guide/Journal for use with Why Shofars Wail in Scripture and Today—
The Exciting Stories and Miracles!   By Mary A. Bruno, Ph.D.

POINTS TO PONDER: (Sharing your answers in class is always optional.)

1. Main characters:

_____

_____

_____

_____

2. Key words:

_____

_____

_____

_____

3. What changed Mary's mind about accompanying Rocco to Italy? What does this reveal about God's involvement in your casual conversations?

_____

_____

_____

_____

_____

_____

_____

_____

Study Guide/Journal for use with Why Shofars Wail in Scripture and Today—
The Exciting Stories and Miracles!   By Mary A. Bruno, Ph.D.

252

4. (Three–part question) Do you think God may have scheduled that "divine appointment" with the woman in a van by the Coke machine? Why? What do you think that God may have had in store for her?

_____

_____

_____

_____

_____

_____

_____

5. What supernatural changes did Rocco and Mary experience after he stepped up and blew the shofar at Council Bluffs, Iowa?

_____

_____

_____

_____

_____

_____

_____

_____

_____

Study Guide/Journal for use with Why Shofars Wail in Scripture and Today—
The Exciting Stories and Miracles!   By Mary A. Bruno, Ph.D.

253

6. (Two–part question) What had the Bruno's been doing daily as they drove across the USA? Why do you think God blessed their relationship (marriage) during this trip?

_____

_____

_____

_____

_____

_____

_____

7. (Two–part question) Do you think the Brunos' attitude about having to change their driving route to Niagara Falls had anything to do with their readiness for God's next "divine appointment" with the (digeridoo) couple? Since God obviously loves and cares about that couple, how do you think He may have followed up on their conversation with the Brunos in the park?

_____

_____

_____

_____

_____

_____

_____

Study Guide/Journal for use with Why Shofars Wail in Scripture and Today—
The Exciting Stories and Miracles!   By Mary A. Bruno, Ph.D.

254

8. (Two–part question) What did the "tea incident" at Boston Harbor reveal about Rocco and Mary's mood after 9 10 days of togetherness on the road? How do you think God felt about their frame of mind?

_____

_____

_____

_____

_____

_____

_____

9. Discuss your special insights regarding how God stays involved with His people, and with those who dare to sound the shofar.

_____

_____

_____

_____

_____

_____

_____

_____

_____

_____

_____

Study Guide/Journal for use with Why Shofars Wail in Scripture and Today—
The Exciting Stories and Miracles!   By Mary A. Bruno, Ph.D.

255

_____

_____

_____

_____

_____

_____

_____

_____

_____

_____

10. Improve your communication skills by summarizing this chapter in twenty–five meaningful words or less.

_____

_____

_____

_____

_____

_____

Dear God, I love and appreciate You because:

_____

_____

_____

Study Guide/Journal for use with Why Shofars Wail in Scripture and Today—
The Exciting Stories and Miracles!　　　　By Mary A. Bruno, Ph.D.

256

PRAYER REQUESTS/POTENTIAL MIRACLES:

"I will answer them before they even call to me.
While they are still talking about their needs,
I will go ahead and answer their prayers!"
(Isaiah 65:24 NLT)

_____
_____
_____
_____
_____
_____
_____
_____
_____
_____
_____
_____
_____
_____
_____
_____
_____
_____

Study Guide/Journal for use with Why Shofars Wail in Scripture and Today—
The Exciting Stories and Miracles!   By Mary A. Bruno, Ph.D.

257

_____

_____

_____

_____

_____

_____

_____

_____

_____

NOTES:

_____

_____

_____

_____

Answers: Chapter 31

1–2. (Opinion)

3. John Welsh said, "Us fellas kind of like to have our wives around when we preach." (p. 219)

4. (Opinions) (pp. 220–221)

5. They enjoyed a greater sense of unity and sweet peace. (p. 222)

6. They were praising God and affirming His ownership of the land as they entered each state along the way. (Opinion) (p. 222)

7. (Opinion) (pp. 223–225)

8. They were having fun. (p. 225) (Opinion)

9–10. (Opinion)

Study Guide/Journal for use with Why Shofars Wail in Scripture and Today—
The Exciting Stories and Miracles!   By Mary A. Bruno, Ph.D.

258

Chapter 32
Shofar Trip – Part 2: Italy

Date: _____

The shofar was mentioned on textbook pages: 227, 228, 229, 230, 231, 232 and 233.

Events or hurdles that you have faced while focusing on this chapter:

_____

_____

_____

_____

_____

_____

_____

_____

___True: ___False:

Prior to attempting this chapter, I have asked God to give me new wisdom and understanding and to reveal all that I need to learn or change at this time.

Study Guide/Journal for use with Why Shofars Wail in Scripture and Today—
The Exciting Stories and Miracles!   By Mary A. Bruno, Ph.D.

259

POINTS TO PONDER: (Sharing your answers in class is always optional.)

1. Main characters:

_____

_____

_____

_____

2. Key words:

_____

_____

_____

_____

3. (Three–part question) What was Caposele's population during the tourist season? Who founded Chiesa Evangelica di Caposele? In what year was the church founded?

_____

_____

_____

_____

_____

_____

_____

Study Guide/Journal for use with Why Shofars Wail in Scripture and Today—
The Exciting Stories and Miracles!   By Mary A. Bruno, Ph.D.

260

4. (Three–part question) While visiting Michela at the hospital, what did Mary feel led to tell her? What did Mary notice when she was climbing the stairs to home? What did Rocco say about that?

_____

_____

_____

_____

_____

_____

_____

_____

_____

_____

_____

5. How did Concetta respond to Rocco's preaching on June 14?

_____

_____

_____

_____

_____

_____

Study Guide/Journal for use with Why Shofars Wail in Scripture and Today—
The Exciting Stories and Miracles!   By Mary A. Bruno, Ph.D.

261

6. (Three–part question) What did Antonietta experience when Mary told her (in English—Mary's native language), how to receive the Lord, while Rocco interpreted her words to Italian, which was Antonietta's native language? Can you think of a place in the Bible where something similar happened? [Hint] See below. Has this happened yet in your ministry or for someone you know?

> And they were all filled with the Holy Spirit and began to speak with other tongues, as the Spirit gave them utterance. And there were dwelling in Jerusalem Jews, devout men, from every nation under heaven. And when this sound occurred, the multitude came together, and were confused, because **everyone heard them speak in his own language.** Then they were all amazed and marveled, saying to one another, "Look, are not all these who speak Galileans? And how *is it that* **we hear, each in our own language in which we were born**? Parthians and Medes and Elamites, those dwelling in Mesopotamia, Judea and Cappadocia, Pontus and Asia, Phrygia and Pamphylia, Egypt and the parts of Libya adjoining Cyrene, **visitors from Rome**, both Jews and proselytes, Cretans and Arabs—**we hear them speaking in our own tongues** the wonderful works of God." So they were all amazed and perplexed, saying to one another, "Whatever could this mean?"
>
> —Acts 2:4–12, emphasis added

_____

_____

_____

_____

_____

_____

_____

_____

_____

_____

Study Guide/Journal for use with Why Shofars Wail in Scripture and Today—
The Exciting Stories and Miracles!   By Mary A. Bruno, Ph.D.

262

7. What happened to Michela after Mary had shared what she was certain that God wanted her to say?

_____

_____

_____

_____

8. After they had blown the shofar, and affirmed God's ownership of the land in three countries, what happened to the divisive walls that had bristled between Rocco and Mary during their many years of marriage?

_____

_____

_____

_____

_____

9. Lessons learned or special insights about the Lord and His loving involvement with His people.

_____

_____

_____

Study Guide/Journal for use with Why Shofars Wail in Scripture and Today—
The Exciting Stories and Miracles!   By Mary A. Bruno, Ph.D.

263

_____

_____

_____

_____

_____

_____

_____

_____

_____

10. Improve your communication skills by summarizing this chapter in twenty–five meaningful words or less.

_____

_____

_____

_____

_____

_____

Dear God, I love and appreciate You because:

_____

_____

_____

Study Guide/Journal for use with Why Shofars Wail in Scripture and Today—
The Exciting Stories and Miracles!   By Mary A. Bruno, Ph.D.

264

PRAYER REQUESTS/POTENTIAL MIRACLES:

"I will answer them before they even call to me.
While they are still talking about their needs,
I will go ahead and answer their prayers!"
(Isaiah 65:24 NLT)

_____
_____
_____
_____
_____
_____
_____
_____
_____
_____
_____
_____
_____
_____
_____
_____
_____
_____
_____
_____

Study Guide/Journal for use with Why Shofars Wail in Scripture and Today—
The Exciting Stories and Miracles! By Mary A. Bruno, Ph.D.

265

_____

_____

_____

_____

_____

_____

_____

NOTES:

_____

_____

_____

_____

Answers: Chapter 32

1–2. (Opinion)

3. Caposele's population reached 3,500 in the tourist season. Pastor Geremia Albano's father founded Chiesa Evangelica di Caposele. The church was founded in 1945. (p. 227)

4. Mary said that God was going to raise Michela up and people would see her new dynamic for God's glory. Mary's back did not hurt. Rocco said it happened to her as it had with Job. God healed him when he prayed for his friends. (p. 228)

5. Concetta jumped up and shouted "Bravo!" (p. 229)

6. Antonietta understood what Mary was saying in English—before Rocco had translated it to Italian. Visitors from Rome (Italians) are included in verse 10 of Acts 2:4–12. (pp. 229–230)

7. Michela got sicker. (pp. 231–232)

8. The walls between them disappeared. (p. 232)

9–10. (Opinion)

Study Guide/Journal for use with Why Shofars Wail in Scripture and Today—
The Exciting Stories and Miracles!   By Mary A. Bruno, Ph.D.

266

Chapter 33

Shofar Trip – Part 3: Southern Route

The shofar was mentioned on textbook pages: 235, 236, 237, and 238.

Events or hurdles that you have faced while focusing on this chapter:

_____

_____

_____

_____

_____

_____

_____

_____

_____

_____

___True: ___False:

Prior to attempting this chapter, I have asked God to give me new wisdom and understanding and to reveal all that I need to learn or change at this time.

Study Guide/Journal for use with Why Shofars Wail in Scripture and Today—
The Exciting Stories and Miracles!   By Mary A. Bruno, Ph.D.

267

POINTS TO PONDER: (Sharing your answers in class is always optional.)

1. Main characters:

_____

_____

_____

_____

2. Key words:

_____

_____

_____

_____

3. (Two-part question) What are your thoughts regarding the Liberty Bell's inscription? Why do you think it is there?

_____

_____

_____

_____

_____

_____

_____

_____

Study Guide/Journal for use with Why Shofars Wail in Scripture and Today—
The Exciting Stories and Miracles!　　　　　　By Mary A. Bruno, Ph.D.

268

4. (Two-part question) How did Mary's shofar blasts by the Liberty Bell affect others in the room? Explain.

_____

_____

_____

_____

_____

_____

_____

5. What happened as Rocco and Mary left the Liberty Bell Center and walked toward their car?

_____

_____

_____

_____

_____

_____

_____

_____

_____

_____

Study Guide/Journal for use with Why Shofars Wail in Scripture and Today—
The Exciting Stories and Miracles!   By Mary A. Bruno, Ph.D.

269

6. What happened when the Brunos got back on the freeway after visiting the Liberty Bell?

_____

_____

_____

_____

_____

_____

_____

_____

_____

_____

7. (Two–part question) Do you think that God was involved in Rocco and Mary's 60–mile route change that led them to meet a young man at a Mexican restaurant in Livingston, Alabama? Tell if anything similar has happened to help you to reach a *divine appointment.*

_____

_____

_____

_____

_____

_____

Study Guide/Journal for use with Why Shofars Wail in Scripture and Today—
The Exciting Stories and Miracles!   By Mary A. Bruno, Ph.D.

270

_____

_____

_____

_____

_____

8. (Four–part question) How does the following passage apply to what Mary told that young man during their encounter? Has God ever given you a "word in season" for anyone? If not, do you want Him to? Please explain.

"The Lord GOD has given Me
The tongue of the learned,
That I should know how to speak
A word in season to *him who is* weary."

(Isa. 50:4)

_____

_____

_____

_____

_____

_____

_____

_____

_____

_____

Study Guide/Journal for use with Why Shofars Wail in Scripture and Today—
The Exciting Stories and Miracles!   By Mary A. Bruno, Ph.D.

271

_____

_____

_____

_____

9. Please comment on your observations from this chapter.

_____

_____

_____

_____

_____

_____

_____

_____

_____

10. Improve your communication skills by summarizing this chapter in twenty–five meaningful words or less.

_____

_____

_____

_____

_____

_____

Study Guide/Journal for use with Why Shofars Wail in Scripture and Today—
The Exciting Stories and Miracles!   By Mary A. Bruno, Ph.D.

272

Dear God, I love and appreciate You because:

_____

_____

_____

PRAYER REQUESTS/POTENTIAL MIRACLES:

"I will answer them before they even call to me.
While they are still talking about their needs,
I will go ahead and answer their prayers!"
(Isaiah 65:24 NLT)

_____

_____

_____

_____

_____

_____

_____

_____

_____

_____

_____

_____

Study Guide/Journal for use with Why Shofars Wail in Scripture and Today—
The Exciting Stories and Miracles!   By Mary A. Bruno, Ph.D.

273

_____

_____

_____

_____

_____

_____

_____

_____

_____

_____

NOTES:

_____

_____

_____

Answers: Chapter 33

1–3. (Opinions) (p. 235)

4. They rejoiced and praised God. Yes. The guard told visitors that the shofar sounded when God established the Day of Jubilee. (p. 236)

5. Mary tripped and fell. An unseen force ground her face into the dirt. (pp. 236–237)

6. Two speeding cars nearly sideswiped both sides of their car. (p. 237)

7–8. (Opinion) (pp. 238–239)

9.–10. (Opinions)

Study Guide/Journal for use with Why Shofars Wail in Scripture and Today—
The Exciting Stories and Miracles!   By Mary A. Bruno, Ph.D.

274

Chapter 34
Shofar Trip – Part 4: Home and Miracles

Date:_____

The shofar was mentioned on textbook pages: 241, 242 and 247.

Events or hurdles that you have faced while focusing on this chapter:

_____

_____

_____

_____

_____

_____

_____

_____

___True: ___False:

Prior to attempting this chapter, I have asked God to give me new wisdom and understanding and to reveal all that I need to learn or change at this time.

Study Guide/Journal for use with Why Shofars Wail in Scripture and Today—
The Exciting Stories and Miracles!   By Mary A. Bruno, Ph.D.

275

POINTS TO PONDER: (Sharing your answers in class is always optional.)

1. Main characters:

_____

_____

_____

_____

2. Key words:

_____

_____

_____

_____

3. Comment on what Rocco and Mary's road trips were like before their shofar-blowing journey.

_____

_____

_____

_____

_____

_____

_____

Study Guide/Journal for use with Why Shofars Wail in Scripture and Today—
The Exciting Stories and Miracles!   By Mary A. Bruno, Ph.D.

276

4. (Two-part question) What changed after the Brunos started blowing the shofar together and praying as a team? What was God was doing within them that was reminiscent of the Jericho incident as they continued to blow the shofar and honor Him?

_____

_____

_____

_____

_____

_____

_____

_____

_____

_____

5. Why do you think Ephesians 3:20-21 became Mary's daily prayer for others?

_____

_____

_____

_____

_____

Study Guide/Journal for use with Why Shofars Wail in Scripture and Today—
The Exciting Stories and Miracles!   By Mary A. Bruno, Ph.D.

277

_____

_____

_____

_____

6. (Two–part question) What was unusual about Mary's vision of Michela? What did God tell her about a 40–day Daniel fast?

_____

_____

_____

_____

_____

_____

_____

_____

_____

7. (Two-part question) What did Mary wonder about when Michaela's doctor said she had two days to live? What did the doctor tell Michela after her test?

_____

_____

_____

_____

_____

Study Guide/Journal for use with Why Shofars Wail in Scripture and Today—
The Exciting Stories and Miracles!   By Mary A. Bruno, Ph.D.

278

_____

_____

_____

_____

_____

_____

8. When his pre-surgery test results showed no gallstones, what did Pastor Geremia tell his doctor?

_____

_____

_____

_____

_____

9. Lessons learned, and insights or comments regarding this chapter.

_____

_____

_____

_____

_____

_____

Study Guide/Journal for use with Why Shofars Wail in Scripture and Today—
The Exciting Stories and Miracles!   By Mary A. Bruno, Ph.D.

279

_____

_____

_____

_____

_____

_____

_____

_____

_____

_____

10. Improve your communication skills by summarizing this chapter in twenty-five meaningful words or less.

_____

_____

_____

_____

_____

_____

Dear God, I love and appreciate You because:

_____

_____

_____

Study Guide/Journal for use with Why Shofars Wail in Scripture and Today—
The Exciting Stories and Miracles!　　　　　By Mary A. Bruno, Ph.D.

280

PRAYER REQUESTS/POTENTIAL MIRACLES:

"I will answer them before they even call to me.
While they are still talking about their needs,
I will go ahead and answer their prayers!"
(Isaiah 65:24 NLT)

_____

_____

_____

_____

_____

_____

_____

_____

_____

_____

_____

_____

_____

_____

_____

_____

_____

*Study Guide/Journal for use with Why Shofars Wail in Scripture and Today—
The Exciting Stories and Miracles!*   By Mary A. Bruno, Ph.D.

_____

_____

_____

_____

_____

NOTES:

_____

_____

_____

_____

_____

Answers: Chapter 34

1–2. Opinion

3. Rocco and Mary's road trips were very stressful. Opinion (pp. 241–242)

4. Their relationship improved (p. 242) (Opinion) God was doing His own tearing down and building up within them. (Opinion)

5. Mary began to pray Ephesians 3:20 for others because of the great things that God had done within them during their trip. (pp. 242–243)

6. Michela's lips did not move, but Mary heard her spirit speaking in English. God told Mary that she did not have time for a 40–day Daniel fast. (p. 243)

7. Mary thought about what God had urged her to tell Michaela. She wondered if she would be branded as a false prophet, and if Rocco's door of ministry in Caposele might close. Michela's doctor said her (formerly deteriorated) pancreas was new. (pp. 244–245)

8. The same God, who healed my wife's pancreas also, healed my gallstones!" (p. 246)

9–10. (Opinion)

Study Guide/Journal for use with Why Shofars Wail in Scripture and Today—
The Exciting Stories and Miracles!   By Mary A. Bruno, Ph.D.

282

Dare to Write a Review!

May God bless you for reading: *STUDY GUIDE/JOURNAL/—FOR USE WITH—Why Shofars Wail in Scripture and Today—The Exciting Stories and Miracles!* Authored by Mary A. Bruno, Ph.D.

If you have enjoyed this book, she would be happy to read your review on www.Amazon.com. She reads and treasures every one.

As Barbara Anne Waite,[16] author of *Elsie's Mountain,* once mentioned, "Many people are unaware of the enormous boost that even a few words from a reader can mean for an author. Every review helps, no matter how brief."

Your comments will not only benefit Dr. Mary A. Bruno and other book lovers but may help to boost sales. God could use your review to help others to find peace with Him, learn to share their faith, and to lift up their voices as shofars.

How to Write a Review—It's Easy!

1. Type, www.amazon.com on your browser.
2. Type, *Mary A. Bruno,* Ph.D. on Amazon's search bar, and then click on the magnifying glass.
3. Click on the book's title.
4. Click on the *customer reviews,* (blue writing), by the yellow rating stars (next to a picture of the book).
5. Read a few of the reviews to get an idea of what goes into one.
6. Click on the (gray) *Write A Customer Review* box, and then complete the *Sign In* box that pops up.
7. Dare to wax eloquent and compose your review with your unique observations and style. (If invited, the Lord might even impart some of His ideas.)

For a writer, knowing that a reader has taken the time to compose a brief comment is equal to having received an extremely generous tip. Thank you!

---

[16] www.barbaraannewaite.com

Study Guide/Journal for use with Why Shofars Wail in Scripture and Today—The Exciting Stories and Miracles!   By Mary A. Bruno, Ph.D.

Study Guide/Journal for use with Why Shofars Wail in Scripture and Today—
The Exciting Stories and Miracles!   By Mary A. Bruno, Ph.D.

284

Bibliography

Resources consulted during research for this book include the following:

Books

The Amplified Bible. Grand Rapids: Zondervan, 1980.

Amplified Bible, Classic Edition (AMPC) Copyright © 1954, 1958, 1962, 1964, 1965, 1987, The Lockman Foundation.

The Chicago Manual of Style, Sixteenth Edition. Chicago: The University of Chicago Press, 2010.

Duffield, Guy P. and Nathaniel M. Van Cleave. *Foundations of Pentecostal Theology*, Los Angeles: L.I.F.E. Bible College, 1987.

Fairbairn, Patrick. *The Typology of Scripture.* Grand Rapids: Zondervan, 1969.

Gaebelein, Frank E., ed. *The Expositor's Bible Commentary*, vol. 8 (Matthew - Luke). Grand Rapids: Zondervan, 1984.

Gower, Ralph. *The New Manners And Customs of Bible Times.* Chicago: Moody Press, 1987.

Habershon, Ada R. *The Study of the Types.* Grand Rapids: Kregel Publications, 1973.

Holdcroft, L. Thomas. *The Pentateuch.* Oakland: Western Book Company, 1966.

The King James Version (KJV). [illegible] from the Holy Bible. King James Version in *Strong's Exhaustive Concordance of the Bible* at the Blue Letter Bible: http://www.blbclassic.org/index. cfm.

New King James Version. Copyright © 1982, Thomas Nelson, Inc.

New Living Translation **(NLT)** *Holy Bible,* New Living Translation, copyright © 1996, 2004, 2015 by Tyndale House Foundation. Tyndale House Publishers Inc., Carol Stream, Illinois 60188.

New Revised Standard Version Bible: Catholic Edition (NRSVCE) New Revised Standard Version Bible: Catholic Edition, copyright © 1989, 1993 the Division of Christian Education of the National Council of the Churches of Christ in the United States of America.

Radmacher, Earl D. *The Nelson Study Bible*, New King James version. Nashville: Thomas Nelson, 1997.

Stern, David H. *Complete Jewish Bible.* Clarksville, MD: Messianic Jewish Resources International, 1998.

Strong, James, LL.D., S.T.D. The New Strong's Exhaustive Concordance of the Bible Nashville, Thomas Nelson Publishers, 1990

Trepp, Leo. *The Complete Book of Jewish Observance.* New York: Behrman House, Inc. and Summit Books, 1980.

Zimmerman, Martha. *Celebrate the Feasts of the Old Testament in Your Own Home or Church.* Minneapolis: Bethany House Publishers, 1981.

Websites Contacted

aJudaica.com. "Shofar Guide." http://www.ajudaica.com/guide_shofar.ph.

biblestudy.org. Search for: "How many pounds in an ephah of flour." http://www.biblestudy.org/beginner/bible-weights-and-measures.html

Arnoldussen, Peg. "Yemenite Shofar Kudu Horn." http://pinebaskets.tripod.com/shofar.html.

Becky. "Cleaning the Shofar." http://answers.yahoo.com/question/index?qid=20080528093839AAsrQpF.

BibleGateway.com. "1 Kings 16." http://www.biblegateway.com/passage/?search=I+Kings+16&version=NASB.

BibleGateway.com. "1 Kings 19." http://www.biblegateway.com/passage/?search=I+Kings+19&version=NASB.

BibleGateway.com. "2 Kings 9." http://www.biblegateway.com/passage/?search=II+Kings+9&version=NASB.

BibleGateway.com. "2 Kings 10." http://www.biblegateway.com/passage/?search=II+Kings+10&version=NASB.

Study Guide/Journal for use with Why Shofars Wail in Scripture and Today— The Exciting Stories and Miracles!   By Mary A. Bruno, Ph.D.

285

BibleGateway.com. "Jehu." http://www.biblegateway.com/quicksearch/?quicksearch=Jehu&qs_version=NASB.

BibleGateway.com. "Nathan." https://www.biblegateway.com/quicksearch/?quicksearch=Nathan&qs_version=NIV.

BibleGateway.com. "Numbers 14." http://www.biblegateway.com/passage/?search=Numbers+14%3A14-45&version =NASB.

BibleGateway.com. "Zadok." http://www.biblegateway.com/quicksearch/?quicksearch=Zadok&qs_version=NASB.

Biblehub.com. 1 Samuel 31:6 So Saul and his three sons and his armor .., http://biblehub.com/1_samuel/31-6.htm

Biblehub.com. Isaiah 6:8 Then I heard the voice of the Lord saying .., http://biblehub.com/isaiah/6-8.htm

Bible Study Daily. Judges 6-7 - Bible Study Daily, http://biblestudydaily.org/judges-6-7/

BlueLetterBible.org. "Abishai." "KJV Search Results for "Abishai"." Blue Letter Bible. https://www.blueletterbible.org//search/search.cfm?Criteria=Abishai&t=KJV#s_primary_0_1

BlueLetterBible.org. "Absalom." "KJV Search Results for "absalom"." Blue Letter Bible. https://www.blueletterbible.org//search/search.cfm?Criteria=absalom&t=KJV#s=s_primary_0_1

BlueLetterBible.org. "Amalek." "KJV Search Results for "amalek"." Blue Letter Bible. https://www.blueletterbible.org//search/search.cfm?Criteria=amalek&t=KJV#s_primary_0_1

BlueLetterBible.org. "ark" (Strong's H727 arown). "H727 - 'arown - Strong's Hebrew Lexicon (KJV)." Blue Letter Bible. https://www.blueletterbible.org//lang/lexicon/lexicon.cfm?Strongs=H727&t=KJV

BlueLetterBible.org. "Be strong and of good courage." "KJV Search Results for "be" AND "strong" AND "and" AND "of" AND "good" AND "courage"." Blue Letter Bible. https://www.blueletterbible.org//search/search.cfm?Criteria=be+strong+and+of+good+courage&t=KJV#s_primary_0_1

BlueLetterBible.org. "Cherubim" (Strong's H3742). "KJV Search Results for "cherubims"." Blue Letter Bible. https://www.blueletterbible.org//search/search.cfm?Criteria=cherubims&t=KJV#s=s_primary_0_1

BlueLetterBible.org. "Cornet." "KJV Search Results for "cornet"." Blue Letter Bible. https://www.blueletterbible.org//search/search.cfm?Criteria=cornet&t=KJV#s=s_primary_0_1

BlueLetterBible.org. "Blast." 1 "KJV Search Results for "blast"." Blue Letter Bible. https://www.blueletterbible.org//search/search.cfm?Criteria=blast&t=KJV#s=s_primary_0_1

BlueLetterBible.org. "Blast" (Strong's H4900 – mashak) "H4900 - mashak - Strong's Hebrew Lexicon (KJV)." Blue Letter Bible. https://www.blueletterbible.org//lang/lexicon/lexicon.cfm?Strongs=H4900&t=KJV

BlueLetterBible.org. "Blow" (Strong's H8628 taqa) "H8628 - taqa` - Strong's Hebrew Lexicon (KJV)." Blue Letter Bible. https://www.blueletterbible.org//lang/lexicon/lexicon.cfm?Strongs=H8628&t=KJV

BlueLetterBible.org. "Clap" (Strong's H8628). "H8628 - taqa` - Strong's Hebrew Lexicon (KJV)." Blue Letter Bible. https://www.blueletterbible.org//lang/lexicon/lexicon.cfm?Strongs=H8628&t=KJV

BlueLetterBible.org. "Cornet" (Strong's H7782). "KJV Search Results for "cornet"." Blue Letter Bible. https://www.blueletterbible.org//search/search.cfm?Criteria=cornet&t=KJV#s=s_primary_0_1

BlueLetterBible.org. "Cornet" Strong's H7162). "H7162 - qeren (Aramaic) - Strong's Hebrew Lexicon (KJV)." Blue Letter Bible. https://www.blueletterbible.org//lang/Lexicon/Lexicon.cfm?Strongs=H7162&t=KJV

BlueLetterBible.org. "Courage" (Strong's H553). "KJV Search Results for "courage"." Blue Letter Bible. https://www.blueletterbible.org//search/search.cfm?Criteria=courage&t=KJV#s=s_primary_0_1

Study Guide/Journal for use with Why Shofars Wail in Scripture and Today—
The Exciting Stories and Miracles!   By Mary A. Bruno, Ph.D.

286

BlueLetterBible.org. "David anointed king." "KJV Search Results for "David" AND "anointed" AND "king"." Blue Letter Bible. https://www.blueletterbible.or g//search/search.cfm?Criteria= David+anointed+king&t=KJV#s =s_primary_0_1

BlueLetterBible.org. "Discomfited." H2522, H3807, H2000, H2729, H4522. "KJV Search Results for "discomfited"." Blue Letter Bible. https://www.blueletterbible.or g//search/search.cfm?Criteria= discomfited&t=KJV#s=s_primar y_0_1

BlueLetterBible.org. "Gihon" (Strong's H1521). "KJV Search Results for "Gihon"." Blue Letter Bible. https://www.blueletterbible.or g//search/search.cfm?Criteria= Gihon&t=KJV#s=s_primary_0_1

BlueLetterBible.org. "God" (Strong's H410). "KJV Search Results for "Gihon"." Blue Letter Bible. https://www.blueletterbible.or g//search/search.cfm?Criteria= Gihon&t=KJV#s=s_primary_0_1

BlueLetterBible.org. "God" (Strong's H426). "H426 - 'elahh (Aramaic) - Strong's Hebrew Lexicon (KJV)." Blue Letter Bible. https://www.blueletterbible.or g//lang/lexicon/lexicon.cfm?Str ongs=H426&t=KJV

BlueLetterBible.org. "God" (Strong's H433). "H433 - 'elowahh - Strong's Hebrew Lexicon (KJV)." Blue Letter Bible. https://www.blueletterbible.or

g//lang/lexicon/lexicon.cfm?Str ongs=H433&t=KJV

BlueLetterBible.org. "God (Strong's H3068). "H3068 - Yĕhovah - Strong's Hebrew Lexicon (KJV)." Blue Letter Bible. https://www.blueletterbible.or g//lang/lexicon/lexicon.cfm?Str ongs=H3068&t=KJV

BlueLetterBible.org. "God" (Strong's G2316). "H3068 - Yĕhovah - Strong's Hebrew Lexicon (KJV)." Blue Letter Bible. https://www.blueletterbible.or g//lang/lexicon/lexicon.cfm?Str ongs=H3068&t=KJV

BlueLetterBible.org. "God" (Strong's G2304). "G2304 - theios - Strong's Greek Lexicon (KJV)." Blue Letter Bible. https://www.blueletterbible.or g//lang/lexicon/lexicon.cfm?Str ongs=G2304&t=KJV

BlueLetterBible.org. "God" (Strong's G2305). "G2305 - theiotēs - Strong's Greek Lexicon (KJV)." Blue Letter Bible. https://www.blueletterbible.or g//lang/lexicon/lexicon.cfm?Str ongs=G2305&t=KJV

BlueLetterBible.org. "God" (Strong's H6697). "H6697 - tsuwr - Strong's Hebrew Lexicon (KJV)." Blue Letter Bible. https://www.blueletterbible.or g//lang/lexicon/lexicon.cfm?Str ongs=H6697&t=KJV

BlueLetterBible.org. "God" (Strong's H3069). "H3069 - Yĕhovih - Strong's Hebrew Lexicon (KJV)." Blue Letter Bible. https://www.b

BlueLetterBible.org. "Hazael" (Strong's H2371), "H2371 - Chaza'el - Strong's Hebrew Lexicon (KJV)." Blue Letter Bible. https://www.blueletterbible.or g//lang/lexicon/lexicon.cfm?Str ongs=H2371&t=KJV

BlueLetterBible.org. "Horn." "KJV Search Results for "horn"." Blue Letter Bible. https://www.blueletterbible.or g//search/search.cfm?Criteria= horn&t=KJV#s=s_primary_0_1

BlueLetterBible.org. "Horn" (Strong's H7161 queren). "H7161 - qeren - Strong's Hebrew Lexicon (KJV)." Blue Letter Bible. https://www.blueletterbible.or g//lang/lexicon/lexicon.cfm?Str ongs=H7161&t=KJV

BlueLetterBible.org. "Horns" (Strong's H7161 queren). "H7161 - qeren - Strong's Hebrew Lexicon (KJV)." Blue Letter Bible. https://www.blueletterbible.or g//lang/lexicon/lexicon.cfm?Str ongs=H7161&t=KJV

BlueLetterBible.org. "Jehovah" (Strong's H3068). "H3068 - Yĕhovah - Strong's Hebrew Lexicon (KJV)." Blue Letter Bible. https://www.blueletterbible.or g//lang/lexicon/lexicon.cfm?Str ongs=H3068&t=KJV

BlueLetterBible.org. "Jehovahjireh" (Strong's H3070). "H3070 - Yĕhovah yireh - Strong's Hebrew Lexicon (KJV)." Blue Letter Bible. https://www.blueletterbible.or g//lang/lexicon/lexicon.cfm?Str ongs=H3070&t=KJV

Study Guide/Journal for use with Why Shofars Wail in Scripture and Today—
The Exciting Stories and Miracles!   By Mary A. Bruno, Ph.D.

287

BlueLetterBible.org. "Jehovahnissi" (Strong's H3071). "H3071 - Yĕhovah nicciy - Strong's Hebrew Lexicon (KJV)." Blue Letter Bible. https://www.blueletterbible.or g//lang/lexicon/lexicon.cfm?Str ongs=H3071&t=KJV

BlueLetterBible.org. "Jehu" (Strong's H3058). "H3058 - Yehuw' - Strong's Hebrew Lexicon (KJV)." Blue Letter Bible. https://www.blueletterbible.or g//lang/lexicon/lexicon.cfm?Str ongs=H3058&t=KJV

BlueLetterBible.org. "Joshua" (Strong's H3091). "H3091 - Yĕhowshuwa` - Strong's Hebrew Lexicon (KJV)." Blue Letter Bible. https://www.blueletterbible.or g//lang/lexicon/lexicon.cfm?Str ongs=H3091&t=KJV

BlueLetterBible.org. "Joshua." "Joshua 1 (KJV) - Now after the death of." Blue Letter Bible. https://www.blueletterbible.or g//kjv/jos/1/1/ss1/s_188001

BlueLetterBible.org. "Joyful" (Strong's H7321). "H7321 - ruwa` - Strong's Hebrew Lexicon (KJV)." Blue Letter Bible. https://www.blueletterbible.or g//lang/lexicon/lexicon.cfm?Str ongs=H7321&t=KJV

BlueLetterBible.org. "Jubile." "KJV Search Results for "Jubile"." Blue Letter Bible. https://www.blueletterbible.or g//search/search.cfm?Criteria=J ubile&t=KJV#s=s_primary_0_1

BlueLetterBible.org. "Jubilee" (Strong's H8643 teruwah). "H8643 - tĕruw`ah - Strong's Hebrew Lexicon (KJV)." Blue Letter Bible. https://www.blueletterbible.or g//lang/lexicon/lexicon.cfm?Str ongs=H8643&t=KJV

BlueLetterBible.org. "Judges 3." "Judges 3 (KJV) - Now these are the nations." Blue Letter Bible. https://www.blueletterbible.or g//kjv/jdg/3/1/ss1/s_214001

BlueLetterBible.org. "Lord" (Strong's H113). "H113 - 'adown - Strong's Hebrew Lexicon (KJV)." Blue Letter Bible. https://www.blueletterbible.or g//lang/lexicon/lexicon.cfm?Str ongs=H113&t=KJV

BlueLetterBible.org. "Lord" (Strong's H135). "H135 - 'Addan - Strong's Hebrew Lexicon (KJV)." Blue Letter Bible. https://www.blueletterbible.or g//lang/lexicon/lexicon.cfm?Str ongs=H135&t=KJV

BlueLetterBible.org. "Lord" Strong's H3050. "H3050 - Yahh - Strong's Hebrew Lexicon (KJV)." Blue Letter Bible. https://www.blueletterbible.or g//lang/lexicon/lexicon.cfm?Str ongs=H3050&t=KJV

BlueLetterBible.org. "Lord" (Strong's H1376). "H1376 - gĕbiyr - Strong's Hebrew Lexicon (KJV)." Blue Letter Bible. https://www.blueletterbible.or g//lang/lexicon/lexicon.cfm?Str ongs=H1376&t=KJV
BlueLetterBible.org. "Lord" (Strong's G1203). G1203 - despotēs - Strong's Greek Lexicon (KJV)." Blue Letter Bible. https://www.blueletterbible.or g//lang/lexicon/lexicon.cfm?Str ongs=G1203&t=KJV

BlueLetterBible.org. "Lord" (Strong's G2962). "G2962 - kyrios - Strong's Greek Lexicon (KJV)." Blue Letter Bible. https://www.blueletterbible.or g//lang/lexicon/lexicon.cfm?Str ongs=G2962&t=KJV

BlueLetterBible.org. "Mercy seat." "KJV Search Results for "Mercy" AND "seat"." Blue Letter Bible. https://www.blueletterbible.or g//search/search.cfm?Criteria= Mercy+seat&t=KJV#s=s_primar y_0_1

BlueLetterBible.org. "Moses minister." "KJV Search Results for "Moses" AND "minister"." Blue Letter Bible. https://www.blueletterbible.or g//search/search.cfm?Criteria= Moses%27+minister&t=KJV#s= s_primary_0_1

BlueLetterBible.org. "Nathan." "KJV Search Results for "Nathan"." Blue Letter Bible. https://www.blueletterbible.or g//search/search.cfm?Criteria= Nathan&t=KJV#s=s_primary_0_ 1

BlueLetterBible.org. "Nehemiah 3:1-32 KJV." "Nehemiah 3 (KJV) - Then Eliashib the high priest." Blue Letter Bible. https://www.blueletterbible.or g//kjv/neh/3/1/ss1/s_416001

BlueLetterBible.org. "Oshea" (Strong's H1954). "H1954 - Howshea` - Strong's Hebrew Lexicon (KJV)." Blue Letter Bible. https://www.blueletterbible.or g//lang/lexicon/lexicon.cfm?Str ongs=H1954&t=KJV

BlueLetterBible.org. "Plagued" (Strong's H6062). "KJV Search Results for "plagued"."

Study Guide/Journal for use with Why Shofars Wail in Scripture and Today—
The Exciting Stories and Miracles!   By Mary A. Bruno, Ph.D.

288

Blue Letter Bible. https://www.blueletterbible.or g//search/search.cfm?Criteria=plaguonv.t=kjv#s=s_primary_0_1

BlueLetterBible.org. "Qeren" (Aramaic - Strong's H7162) "H7162 - qeren (Aramaic) - Strong's Hebrew Lexicon (KJV)." Blue Letter Bible. https://www.blueletterbible.or g//lang/lexicon/lexicon.cfm?Str ongs=H7162&t=KJV

BlueLetterBible.org. "Was rent"(Strong's G4977) in Matthew 27:51. "KJV Search Results for "Was" AND "rent"."

Blue Letter Bible. https://www.blueletterbible.or g//search/search.cfm?Criteria= Was+rent&t=KJV#s=s_primary_ 0_1

BlueLetterBible.org. "rhēma" "G4487 - rhēma - Strong's Greek Lexicon (KJV)." Blue Letter Bible. Accessed 9 Jun, 2016. https://www.blueletterbible.or g//lang/Lexicon/Lexicon.cfm?St rongs=G4487&t=KJV

BlueLetterBible.org. "Saul." "KJV Search Results for "Saul"." Blue Letter Bible. https://www.blueletterbible.or g//search/search.cfm?Criteria= Saul&t=KJV#s=s_primary_0_1

BlueLetterBible.org. "Shophar" (Strong's 7782) "H7782 - showphar - Strong's Hebrew Lexicon (KJV)." Blue Letter Bible. https://www.blueletterbible.or g//lang/lexicon/lexicon.cfm?Str ongs=H7782&t=KJV

BlueLetterBible.org. "Sing"(Strong's H7442). "KJV Search Results for "Sing"." Blue Letter Bible https://www.blueletterbible.or g//search/search.cfm?Criteria= Sing&t=KJV#s=s_primary_0_1

BlueLetterBible.org. "Trumpet" "G4537 - salpizō - Strong's Greek Lexicon (KJV)." Blue Letter Bible. https://www.blueletterbible.or g//lang/lexicon/lexicon.cfm?Str ongs=G4537&t=KJV

BlueLetterBible.org. "Water gate" (Strong's H4325). "H4325 - mayim - Strong's Hebrew Lexicon (KJV)." Blue Letter Bible. https://www.blueletterbible.or g//lang/lexicon/lexicon.cfm?Str ongs=H4325&t=KJV

BlueLetterBible.org. "Yowbel" (Strong's H3104). "H3104 - yowbel - Strong's Hebrew Lexicon (KJV)." Blue Letter Bible. https://www.blueletterbible.or g//lang/lexicon/lexicon.cfm?Str ongs=H3104&t=KJV

Brix, Shawn. "The Final Sacrifice." Today 61, no. 2, March/April 2011 (Palos Heights, Illinois: ReFrame Media, a division of Back to God Ministries International). http://today.reframemedia.com /archives/the-final-sacrifice-2011-04-22. Used by permission.

Conservapedia.com. "Shofar." www.conservapedia.com/Shofa r.

Crivoice.org. "Hebrew Calendar of the Old Testament."

http://www.crivoice.org/calend ar.html.

Funn, Foruho "Decoding the Shofar." http://www.myjewishlearning.c om/article/decoding-the-shofar/.

Hubpages.com. In Florida how many lies does it take to make a Conspiracy?, http://hubpages.com/politics/I n-Florida-how-many-lies-does-it-take-to-make-a-Con

I grandi condottieri (1965) - IMDb, http://www.imdb.com/title/tt0 060570/

In Touch. Cease Striving - In Touch, https://www.intouch.org/read/ magazine/daily-devotions/cease-striving

ISC Netherlands. PRAYERS FOR THE LORD'S MERCY - ISC Netherlands, http://www.iscnetherlands.nl/d ownloads/prayer.doc

jashow.org. How to Become a Christian - how to have eternal life .., https://www.jashow.org/how-to-become-a-christian

Kavanaugh, Ellen "Yom Teruah· Day of The Shofar Blast." http://www. lightofmashiach.org/yomteruah. html.

lbctruthforlife.org. JOSHUA Joshua s life Before the Conquest - lbctruthforlife.org, http://www.lbctruthforlife.org/ wpcontent/uploads/2015/06/T RUTH-FOR-LIFE-Joshua

Leroe, Robert. Aaron & Hur sermon, Aaron & Hur sermon by Robert Leroe

Study Guide/Journal for use with Why Shofars Wail in Scripture and Today—
The Exciting Stories and Miracles!   By Mary A. Bruno, Ph.D.

289

..,http://www.sermoncentral.com/sermons/aaron--hur-robert-leroe-sermon-on-encourage

lowpc.org. Restoration of Davidic Praise: 7 Hebrew Words for Praise ..,
http://lowpc.org/files/media/newsong/2014/4-27 14%20Hebrew%20Words%20for%20Prais
Mirror Match.
mirror match - @arcaneadagio, http://arcaneadagio.tumblr.com/

Orthodox Union. "How to Blow the Shofar."
http://www.ou.org/news/article/how_to_blow_the_shofar.

Quia. "Rosh Hashanah – The Sounds of the Shofar."
http://www.quia.com/cz/14175.html.

PBS. PRESSURES WITHIN AND WITHOUT SERIES: THE MESSAGE OF NEHEMIAH,
https://www.pbc.org/system/message_files/7758/4615.pdf

Richman, Chaim. "The Meaning Behind the Sounding of the Shofar."
http://www.lttn.org/R3_Article2_MeaningOfShofar.htm.

R. Jones' articles at http://www.talkjesus.com/devotionals/17945-12-gates-jerusalem.html.

Shofar Be Tzion Ministries. "Learn the Shofar."
http://www.shofarbetzion.com/learn_ofarError! Bookmark not defined..htm. Send mail to diane.chester@sbcglobal.net

with questions or comments about this website
Shofar Be Tzion Ministries.
"Shofar Scriptures." Send mail to diane. chester@sbcglobal.net with questions or comments about this website (http://www.shofarbetzion.com/).

Shofar.co. "Shofar News/Articles."
http://www.shofar.co/?item=90&section=170.Shofar-Sounders.com.
"Frequently Asked Questions."
http://www.shofarsounders.com/sh_scents2.html.

Shulman, Mark. "Blasts from the Past, Present and Future: Many Horns, One Voice."
http://beitsimcha.org**Error! Bookmark not defined.**/demoSite/s_ser/Mark-Blasts.asp.

Studylight.org. NLV - Joshua 5:13 - When Joshua was by Jericho, he looked ..,
https://www.studylight.org/bible/nlv/joshua/5-13.html

The Rain. APPENDIX 59. THE TWELVE GATES OF JERUSALEM (NEH. CHS. 3 ..,
http://www.therain.org/appendixes/app59.html

Truth Seekers Ministries - The Potter's House: A lesson on ..,
http://www.truthseekersministries.org/index.php/8-general-articles/49-the-potter
ucg.org.

Examining Ourselves Before the Passover - ucg.org,
http://www.ucg.org/sermons/examining-ourselves-before-the-passover

W., Lisa. "Feast of Trumpets," blog entry, September 2, 2007.
http://followingtheancientpaths.wordpress.com/2007/09/02/yomteruah-2007/.
Wikihow.com. "How to Blow a Shofar."
http://www.wikihow.com/Blow-a-Shofar.

Wikipedia. "Liberty Bell."
http://en. wikipedia.org/wiki/Liberty_Bell

Wikipedia. Va'eira - Wikipedia, the free encyclopedia,
https://en.wikipedia.org/wiki/Va%27eira

Wikipedia. "Shofar."
http://en.wiki pedia.org/wiki/shofar.

Williams, Kevin. "The Call of the Shofar."
http://www.pneumafoundation.org/article.jsp?article=article_kw02.xml.

Wordpress.com. when Joshua was first mentioned in Bible « THE CHURCH OF
..,https://churchofphiladelphia.wordpress.com/tag/when-joshua-was-first-mentioned-i

Wordpress.com. The Word Made Flesh: Real Life Meets Real Truth | Just ..,
https://twmf.wordpress.com/
van Zuijlekom, Denijs. "The Twelve Gates of Jerusalem."
http://www. levendwater.org**Error! Bookmark not defined.**/companion/append59.html.

Study Guide/Journal for use with Why Shofars Wail in Scripture and Today—
The Exciting Stories and Miracles!   By Mary A. Bruno, Ph.D.

Index

Study Guide/Journal for use with Why Shofars Wail in Scripture and Today—
The Exciting Stories and Miracles!   By Mary A. Bruno, Ph.D.

291

D

dancing · 207
dark spirits · 150
David · 155, 157, 158, 162, 167, 170, 172, 173, 174, 178, 182, 186, 285
David wore · 157, 162
Day of Atonement · 84, 90
death squad · 242
Deut. 32:4 · 9
Deut. 32:4, 15, 18, 30, 31; Isa. 17:10; 26:10; 32:12; 51:1 · 93
die · 242
Discomfit · 98
divination · 150
divine appointment · 12, 253, 254, 270
divine breath · 86
dogs · 191, 194

E

Eagles' Wings · xiii
earth · 60, 68, 231, 234, 236, 237, 239, 242
earthquake · 234
effeminate · 245
Egypt · 38, 60, 114, 262
Ehud · 127, 130
El · 9
Elijah · 187, 188, 189, 194
Elijah's juniper tree · 188
Elisha · 194
Elohim · 9
Elyon · 9
enemy · 72, 76, 93, 98, 127, 130, 134, 142, 146, 221, 226
English · 262, 266, 282
engrave · 63
ephah · 285
Ephesians 2:4-8 · 182
Ephesians 6:17 · 141
ephod of linen · 162

escort · 162, 178
Ex, 3:13–15 · 9
Ex. 15:26, I Cor. 12:9 · 9
Ex. 17:15, Ex. 17:8–15 · 9
Ex. 17:6 · 93
Ex. 17:6; Deut. 32:4, 15, 18, 30, 31; Isa. 17:10; 26:10; 32:12; 51:1; Ps. 19:14; 1 Cor. 10:4. · 9
Exodus 17:9–16 · 98
Exodus 19:13 · 49
Exodus 19:9 · 48
Exodus 24:13 · 98
experience · 20, 149, 158, 236, 253, 262
experimented · 150
Ez. 48:35, Heb. 13:5, 6 · 10
Ezekiel 33:1-6 · 220

F

faith · 68, 114, 118, 122, 283, 297, 303
false gods · 44
family · 57, 86, 110, 114, 122, 149, 158, 191
fast · 36, 222, 223, 226, 278, 282
fast and pray · 222
fasting · 197, 198, 202, 222
fear · 12, 18, 154
fighting men · 114, 117, 140
financial · 7
fire · 52, 70, 71, 231, 234, 242
Fire · 76
first · xiii, 3, 54, 55, 60, 82, 90, 236
First Thessalonians 4:16–17 · 234
flesh probers · 21
fleshly shofar wails · 148
fornicators · 245
fortunetellers · 150
fourth angel · 238
freeway · 270

G

gag order · 116
gallstones · 279, 282
Gen 17:1 · 9
Gen. 1:1 · 9
Gen. 14:18–20 · 9
Gen. 15:1, 2 · 9
Gen. 2:4 · 9
Gen. 21:33 · 9
Gen. 22:14, Rom. 8:32 · 9
Gideon · 131, 133, 134, 135, 138, 139, 140, 141, 142, 143, 146, 148, 154
glory · xiv, 10, 44, 98, 266
God · vii, xiii, xiv, 1, 3, 4, 5, 6, 7, 9, 10, 11, 12, 13, 14, 15, 16, 17, 18, 19, 20, 21, 22, 23, 24, 25, 26, 27, 29, 30, 33, 34, 36, 37, 38, 39, 40, 41, 42, 43, 44, 45, 46, 47, 48, 50, 52, 53, 56, 57, 58, 60, 61, 62, 63, 64, 65, 66, 68, 69, 70, 71, 72, 73, 74, 76, 77, 79, 81, 82, 83, 87, 88, 90, 91, 93, 94, 96, 98, 99, 100, 102, 103, 105, 106, 107, 108, 109, 110, 111, 112, 114, 115, 117, 120, 122, 123, 124, 125, 126, 127, 129, 130, 131, 133, 134, 135, 136, 137, 138, 139, 140, 144, 146, 147, 149, 150, 151, 152, 154, 155, 157, 158, 160, 162, 163, 165, 168, 171, 173, 175, 176, 179, 183, 184, 186, 187, 188, 189, 191, 192, 194, 195, 197, 198, 200, 202, 203, 204, 205, 208, 210, 211, 213, 214, 215, 216, 218, 219, 220, 222, 224, 226, 227, 228, 230, 231, 232, 234, 235, 240, 242, 243, 245, 247, 248, 250, 251, 253, 254, 255, 256, 258, 259,

Study Guide/Journal for use with Why Shofars Wail in Scripture and Today— The Exciting Stories and Miracles!   By Mary A. Bruno, Ph.D.

292

Study Guide/Journal for use with Why Shofars Wail in Scripture and Today—
The Exciting Stories and Miracles!   By Mary A. Bruno, Ph.D.

293

Study Guide/Journal for use with Why Shofars Wail in Scripture and Today—
The Exciting Stories and Miracles!   By Mary A. Bruno, Ph.D.

294

Study Guide/Journal for use with Why Shofars Wail in Scripture and Today—
The Exciting Stories and Miracles!
By Mary A. Bruno, Ph.D.

295

Study Guide/Journal for use with Why Shofars Wail in Scripture and Today—
The Exciting Stories and Miracles!   By Mary A. Bruno, Ph.D.

296

How to Order

STUDY GUIDE/JOURNAL—FOR USE WITH—
Why Shofars Wail in Scripture and Today—
The Exciting Stories and Miracles!

Authored by Mary A. Bruno, Ph.D.

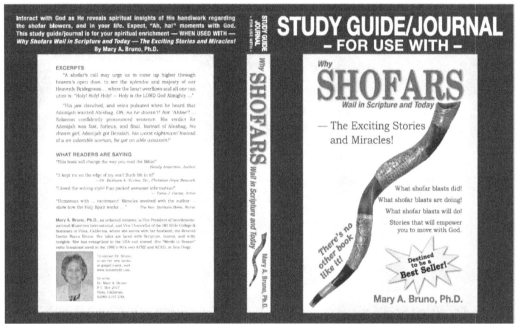

ISBN 978-1535012584 ~~$17.99~~ **$14.99** U.S. Dollars + Tax, S&H within Cont'l. U.S.
Dr. Bruno's unsigned books are available at <u>www.amazon.com</u>

Ask for a signed copy of this book and Dr. Bruno's other writings, at
www.ministrylit.com.

Email: imibcs@aol.com
Write: **Dr. Mary A. Bruno**
P.O. Box 2107
Vista, California 92085-2107 United States of America

Study Guide/Journal for use with Why Shofars Wail in Scripture and Today—
The Exciting Stories and Miracles!   By Mary A. Bruno, Ph.D.

How to Order

Why Shofars Wail in Scripture and Today—
The Exciting Stories and Miracles!
Authored by Mary A. Bruno, Ph.D.

ISBN: 97810997668148

~~$17.99~~ **$14.99** US Dollars. (322 – 6"x9" pages. Paperback),
Ebook $9.99 US Dollars (Kindle)

Order Today! At www.amazon.com and kindle.com.
For Signed books email: imibcs@aol.com

Or write: **Dr. Mary A. Bruno**
              P.O. Box 2107
              Vista, California 92085-2107   United States of America

Study Guide/Journal for use with Why Shofars Wail in Scripture and Today—
The Exciting Stories and Miracles!   By Mary A. Bruno, Ph.D.

How to Order in *LARGE PRINT*

Why Shofars Wail in Scripture and Today (LARGE PRINT) —The Exciting Stories and Miracles!

Authored by Mary A. Bruno, Ph.D.

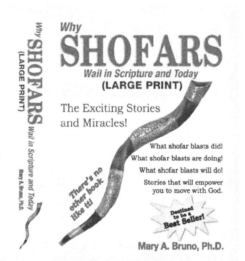

ISBN: 9780997668162 ~~$25.99~~ **$18.99** U.S. Dollars + Tax, S&H within Cont'l. U.S. (630 – 8 ½" x 11" pages. Paperback) **Also available in Braille.**

Easy-to-read print with lots of white space between the lines! (Actual size)

Order Today! at www.amazon.com and kindle.com.
For signed books, email: imibcs@aol.com

    Or write:
**Dr. Mary A. Bruno
P.O. Box 2107
Vista, California 92085-2107**   United States of America

Study Guide/Journal for use with Why Shofars Wail in Scripture and Today— The Exciting Stories and Miracles!   By Mary A. Bruno, Ph.D.

How to Order
How to Make Godly Choices
—Tips for Terrific Results!
Authored by Mary A. Bruno, Ph.D.

Very Easy to Read!
Great for bi-lingual booklovers.

Practical, godly tools to bring matters into focus so the reader can weigh facts and make wise and informed choices that deliver excellent results over a lifetime.
Readers will be challenged to memorize 100 selected Scripture verses that are included.
ISBN-13: 978-1729803400
Order Today! $10.99 U.S. Dollars + tax, S&H within Cont'l. U.S.

Buy one for yourself and one for a friend!

See this book and Dr. Bruno's other writings at www.ministrylit.com.
"Like us" Ministry Lit on Facebook!

Request autographed copies of this and Dr. Bruno's other writings, at www.ministrylit.com.
Her (unsigned) books are also available at www.amazon.com.

Email: imibcs@aol.com
Write: **Dr. Mary A. Bruno**
            P.O. Box 2107
            Vista, California 92085-2107   United States of America

Study Guide/Journal for use with Why Shofars Wail in Scripture and Today—
The Exciting Stories and Miracles!   By Mary A. Bruno, Ph.D.

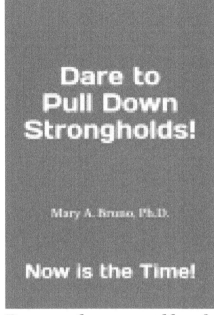
Study Guide/Journal for use with Why Shofars Wail in Scripture and Today—
The Exciting Stories and Miracles!   By Mary A. Bruno, Ph.D.

To request autographed copies of Dr. Bruno's writings,
email imihw'a@aol.com
Or Write:
Mary A. Bruno, Ph.D.
P.O. Box 2107
Vista, California 92085-2107   United States of America

How to Donate *Choices & Strongholds* (*Two Companion Books in One!*)

Authored by Mary A. Bruno, Ph.D.
\Adults and teens in jails, prisons, juvenile halls, or recovery homes, and our heroic veterans, need God's help and guidance.

ISBN: 9780997668124

Your gift can change lives.
Mail your gift to:
Interdenominational Ministries International (IMI)
P.O. Box 2107
Vista, California 92085-2107   United States of America

IMI is a Tax-Exempt 501(C)(3) Non-profit Organization.
Your entire gift marked *"Books"* will be used solely to donate these encouraging and life-changing books.

Study Guide/Journal for use with Why Shofars Wail in Scripture and Today—
The Exciting Stories and Miracles!   By Mary A. Bruno, Ph.D.

303

For Speaking Engagements

 **Dr. Mary A. Bruno,** an ordained minister and published author, serves with her husband, the Reverend Doctor Rocco Bruno. She is Co-founder/Vice President of Interdenominational Ministries International, and Co-founder/Vice Chancellor of IMI Bible College and Seminary in Vista, California.

She has earned a Ministerial Diploma from L.I.F.E. Bible College; a Master of Theology, and Doctor of Ministry Degree from School of Bible Theology, which awarded her the Honorary Doctor of Divinity Degree. She earned a Doctor of Theology Degree, from IMI Bible College & Seminary; and Doctor of Philosophy Degree in Pastoral Christian Counseling from Evangelical Theological Seminary.

Her talks include humor, witty insights, and Scripture. She has preached in the United States of America, West Indies, Mexico, and abroad. Turnouts skyrocketed when she presided over the Vista Women's Aglow. Her "Words in Season" radio broadcast aired in the 1980's and 90's over KPRZ and KCEO in San Diego County.

Watch for her next book release at www.ministrylit.com.

Also available at www.amazon.com and kindle.com.

Visit the website at www.ministrylit.com.

To contact Dr. Bruno: Email: imibcs@aol.com
Or write:
Dr. Mary A. Bruno
P.O. Box 2107
Vista, California 92085-2107   United States of America

V89-100118-326P-111820

Study Guide/Journal for use with Why Shofars Wail in Scripture and Today—
The Exciting Stories and Miracles!   By Mary A. Bruno, Ph.D.

Study Guide/Journal for use with Why Shofars Wail in Scripture and Today—
The Exciting Stories and Miracles!   By Mary A. Bruno, Ph.D.

305

Study Guide/Journal for use with Why Shofars Wail in Scripture and Today—
The Exciting Stories and Miracles!   By Mary A. Bruno, Ph.D.

306

Made in United States
North Haven, CT
07 October 2021